D1011602

Breaking New Ground

ALSO BY LESTER R. BROWN

*Full Planet, Empty Plates: The
New Geopolitics of Food Scarcity*

*World on the Edge: How to
Prevent Environmental and
Economic Collapse*

Plan B (series)

*Outgrowing the Earth:
The Food Security Challenge in
an Age of Falling Water Tables
and Rising Temperatures*

The Earth Policy Reader
(with Janet Larsen and Bernie
Fischlowitz-Roberts)

*Eco-Economy: Building an
Economy for the Earth*

*State of the World,
annual 1984–2000*
(project director and senior author)

*Vital Signs: The Trends That
Are Shaping Our Future,
annual 1992–2000*

*Beyond Malthus: Nineteen
Dimensions of the Population
Challenge* (with Gary Gardner
and Brian Halweil)

*Tough Choices: Facing
the Challenge of Food Scarcity*

*Who Will Feed China?
Wake-Up Call for a Small Planet*

*Full House: Reassessing the
Earth's Population Carrying
Capacity* (with Hal Kane)

Saving the Planet
(with Christopher Flavin and
Sandra Postel)

Building a Sustainable Society

Running on Empty (with Colin
Norman and Christopher Flavin)

The Twenty-Ninth Day

By Bread Alone
(with Erik Eckholm)

In the Human Interest

World Without Borders

Man and His Environment: Food
(with Gail Finsterbusch)

Seeds of Change

Increasing World Food Output

Man, Land and Food

Breaking New Ground

A PERSONAL HISTORY
Lester R. Brown

Lester R Brown

W. W. NORTON & COMPANY

NEW YORK   •   LONDON

For information about permission
to reproduce selections from this book,
write to Permissions, W. W. Norton & Company, Inc.,
500 Fifth Avenue, New York, NY 10110

For information about special discounts for bulk purchases,
please contact W. W. Norton Special Sales
at specialsales@wwnorton.com or 800-233-4830

Manufacturing by Courier Westford
Book design by Brooke Koven
Production manager: Louise Mattarelliano

ISBN 978-0-393-24006-1

W. W. Norton & Company, Inc.
500 Fifth Avenue, New York, N.Y. 10110
www.wwnorton.com

W. W. Norton & Company Ltd.
Castle House, 75/76 Wells Street, London W1T 3QT

1 2 3 4 5 6 7 8 9 0

Dedication

To my brother and sister,
Carl and Marion.

To my son and daughter,
Brian and Brenda.

And to my grandchildren,
Bridget, Lena, and Cash.

Contents

Preface

Writing an autobiography means asking a lot of questions. Who am I? What have I done? Who were the people and what were the circumstances that shaped my evolution as a person? How did I get where I am? Why am I even writing this book?

To start with the last question, the idea of doing an autobiography was initially suggested by the late Iva Ashner at W. W. Norton & Company perhaps 20 years ago. More recently, Amy Cherry of Norton again raised the question. I was skeptical. It was not at all obvious to me how the world would be better off if I wrote about my life.

Then over dinner one night in the fall of 2010, a longtime friend, syndicated columnist Georgie Anne Geyer, brought the issue up. "You should write an autobiography," she said. "It will help people to better understand not only what you think but also why you think as you do." That dinner discussion was the tipping point. When I brought up the question at our annual board meeting in December 2011 and everyone heartily endorsed the idea, that nailed it.

Writing an autobiography is an exercise in self-psychoanalysis. And it is a tricky business because we rely heavily on memory to reconstruct our past. But as the *New York Times'* Joseph Lelyveld noted, after some autobiographical writing of his own, "We reshape our memories all the time, constantly editing them for our own psychic comfort."

And so we do. In looking at the book in final draft, I realize it is, with one notable exception, about successes. Is this because it is psychically comforting or because my life actually has been largely a string of successes? Lelyveld would probably say that this book reflects my psychic comfort. And he is probably right.

Nonetheless I have tried to capture the essence of a life that began in the midst of the Great Depression and coincided with a period of change unprecedented in human history. It is also a life that has taken me to the earth's far corners, letting me see the world as few have been able to do. It has enabled me both to live in villages on the far side of the planet and to dine with heads of state. The purpose of writing this book is to share these experiences with you.

Breaking New Ground

1

Breakthrough

On a cold evening in late December 1963, I arrived at the train station in Cheyenne, Wyoming, to head home to Washington, DC. My wife, Shirley, and her parents, along with our three-year-old son, Brian, were with me. After a week celebrating Christmas on her folks' ranch, we decided that Shirley and Brian would stay with them for an additional week.

The first thing we saw as we entered the station was the January 6 issue of *U.S. News & World Report.* The cover story was "Why Hunger is to be the World's No. 1 Problem." Shirley and I were stunned. The four-page feature article summarized the principal findings of *Man, Land and Food: Looking Ahead at World Food Needs*, a study I wrote as a junior analyst in the U.S. Department of Agriculture (USDA). Shirley's parents did not know quite what to make of our reaction.

The study contained the first comprehensive projections of world food, population, and cropland to the end of the century. "For the first time," *U.S. News & World Report* said, "a careful study of world food supplies has been matched with the facts of expanding world population. The conclusion: in most of the world, creeping hunger looms." The magazine noted the threat posed by growing human numbers to future food security by quoting the study: "Man has scarcely begun to assess their long-term impact."

On the train headed eastward, crossing Nebraska and then Iowa, I tried to imagine the effect of the study. It was a breakthrough, that was certain. Beyond that I could not visualize exactly how it would affect me personally, at the age of twenty-nine, or the role that it might play in the world. It was clear, however, that my supervisors could no longer think of me as just one of a group of thirty-two "junior professionals" in the Foreign Agricultural Service (FAS) of the USDA.

In *Man, Land and Food* I stated that India's population was projected to expand by 187 million over the next fifteen years. During this period India would have to find a way to feed an added population equal to that of the United States. I concluded that "the old equilibrium between [births and deaths] has been destroyed, but a new equilibrium has not yet been developed. That the current disequilibrium cannot continue indefinitely is certain. Until a new balance is created, however, man must seek to accelerate growth in the supply of food to match the increase in numbers."

The study highlighted the Soviet farm problems that were forcing Soviet Premier Nikita Khrushchev to divert money from guns to butter. The centrally planned and managed farm sector was plagued with inefficiencies. During the 1930s, North American grain exports lagged behind those from Latin America and were barely equal to those of the Soviet Union. But during and after World War II, U.S. agriculture began to find itself. By 1960, the United States and Canada were together exporting 39 million tons of grain, already starting to dominate world grain trade. I projected that this would reach 94 million tons by the end of the century, making North America the world's breadbasket. (In 2000, it turned out, the United States and Canada together exported over 100 million tons of grain.) My study took advantage of the 1958 U.N. population projections, the first to project population growth both by country and for the entire world to the end of the century, thus providing a glimpse of a future that no one had envisioned before.

The origins of *Man, Land and Food* provide some insight into how to succeed in a bureaucracy. When I joined the Asia Branch of the FAS on June 1, 1959, I was assigned the Rice Bowl countries. I was responsible for tracking agricultural developments in Burma (Myanmar), Thailand, Cambodia, Laos, and Vietnam. My very first publication was a modest four-page agricultural circular on the rice situation in Burma.

As my supervisors realized that my interests and knowledge went beyond these few countries, they broadened my research and writing assignments. Next came "The Japanese Agricultural Economy," a thirty-page monograph assessing Japan's potential as a market for U.S. farm products. Shortly after that I was promoted to regional economist and produced a somewhat more ambitious monograph, "An Economic Analysis of Far Eastern Agriculture."

By this point, two years in, I was pretty much on track, although I struggled early on, trying to adjust to the bureaucracy. I had come from a farm where I was my own boss and spent almost all of my time out of doors. Now I was confined to an office dealing with a bureaucratic structure unlike anything I had known before.

Did I ever adjust totally? Probably not. I was always looking for small ways to challenge the establishment. One opportunity arose a few months after President Kennedy took office. In the transition from the Eisenhower administration, our division was upgraded and shifted from the FAS to the newly created Economic Research Service (ERS). In this transition, both the branch and assistant branch chief moved up one grade on the civil service scale. Until then, only our branch chief qualified for office carpeting. But after the upgrade, the assistant branch chief also qualified. They could then carpet both offices and the shared space occupied by their secretaries. As the new carpet was being installed, the nearly new existing carpet in the office of our branch chief was removed, rolled up, and left in the hall.

Sensing an opportunity, I approached my officemates, both of whom were also junior professionals, and said, "Why don't we wait until lunchtime and then get that carpet and install it in our office? We'll explain that we feared it would be discarded and didn't want to see it wasted." One of my officemates, Bill Hall, would have nothing to do with it and went to the library to work. The other, Stuart Lerner, was taken with the idea. So when the workers were at lunch, the two of us dragged the carpet to our office and proceeded to move the three desks and several filing cabinets around until we had it appropriately placed and well anchored.

Late that afternoon when the workers were preparing to leave, they took inventory and realized there was a piece of carpet missing. Someone tipped them off. When they came to our office they calmly explained that the carpet would not be discarded but needed to go back to Central Inventory. Apparently there was a point system. You had to be a senior official to get carpeting and we didn't even register on their eligibility scale. "Well," we said, "we're very busy right now, working on a deadline, and can't be interrupted." Knowing that would not hold them for long, Stuart and I made sure that one or the other of us was in the office from 7 a.m. to 7 p.m. each day, literally sitting on the carpet, while the workers were in the building. After a couple of weeks they gave up. Now we were important!

Although my official responsibilities were in the Asia branch, my personal goal from day 1 at the USDA was to get to know world agriculture. I wanted to be the department's leading authority on the subject.

After two years at the USDA I took a nine-month academic leave in 1961–62 to work on a master's in public administration at the Littauer School of Public Administration, now the Kennedy School of Government, at Harvard. This was an intense program of courses, mostly in economics. By far my favorite course was the graduate seminar in economic development. My term paper was entitled "Agricultural Diversification and Economic Development in Thailand." Perhaps even more important than the courses I took were the other students I got to talk with and know in the Littauer building coffee lounge and the Harkness Commons, a cafeteria where graduate students gathered for meals.

Upon my return to the FAS at the end of May 1962, Quentin West, our very progressive branch chief, called me in to discuss an idea for a new project. He said that we needed some long-term supply and demand projections for Asian agriculture and he wanted me to do them. I agreed that this would be useful, but noted that it is impossible to project import and export trends for a region in isolation. If you do not know the conditions elsewhere in the world, you will not know with certainty whether a given commodity will be flowing into or out of the region. After going back and forth on this for a while, the meeting came to an end.

A week or so later, Quentin again called me in and tried to make the case that we could do the region by itself. I replied that this approach would not work. A few days later, I was called in yet again. This time he changed the question: "Could you do agricultural supply and demand projections for the world?" "Yes," I said without hesitation. Quentin, who had a PhD in economics from Cornell, asked if I could do it in six months—that is, by the end of 1962. Again, I said yes.

I went to work day and night with strong support from our senior statistical clerk, Edith Allen, who gathered and organized the data. Early in this process I devised a world grain model, with the world divided into seven geographic areas, as the framework for the study. To save time, I frequently spent the night at the office, working until 1 or 2 a.m. and then sleeping until 6 a.m. Since there was no comfortable place in my office to sleep, I would go down the hall to the office of the administrator, Nate Koffsky, and—unbeknownst to him—sleep on his leather couch. My great fear was that one day I would oversleep and he would discover me. Although Nate was a friend and a remarkably good-natured guy, I did not relish the prospect of being found asleep on his couch. Fortunately, it never happened.

In late December, I presented Quentin with a manuscript. He reviewed it and made a few minor suggestions. I reworked it and within a few days everything was wrapped up and ready to go. After a final read, Quentin sent the manuscript to our division director, Wilhelm Anderson, to forward it for publication. That's when the road got rough.

Wilhelm, someone for whom I had a lot of respect and affection, was—there is no other way to say it—flabbergasted. He called Quentin into his office and said he could not approve my manuscript for publication. "If I send it forward, every branch chief in our division will be on my back. I'll have a revolution on my hands. You have done a study covering their regions that they were not consulted on and did not even know about."

By then I felt the only option was to look for a commercial

publisher. But before I could do that, Wilhelm summoned Quentin into his office again and said, "I am going on vacation in a few weeks and will appoint you acting division director. If you then want to approve this study and forward it for publication, it's your problem."

Quentin could not have been more pleased. He sent it forward during his first day. But instead of following a direct line to the Government Printing Office, those above the division level thought it needed additional clearances because of its sheer scope and also because it discussed population—something no one talked about in government in those days. In addition, it was written by a little-known junior staffer.

Although it took only six months to research and write the study, it took some nine months to get it cleared. It was finally approved for publication by John Schnittker, then leader of the staff economics group. John himself told me about this final crucial step only a few years ago: He had made a conscious decision not to send the report to the secretary before publication.

Once it had been cleared for printing, I was not willing to rely solely on the Office of Information to publicize the findings and decided to do further outreach of my own. Because *U.S. News & World Report* was much more prone to using graphics and numbers than other weekly news magazines, I brashly called David Lawrence, its founder-editor. I did not get through to him but was connected to John Howard, an agricultural reporter.

I described the study and offered to share the contents with him. John was interested and came by the office where I had one of the seven carbon copies, bound in a three-ring binder, replete with graphs and tables. We went through it and after talking about it at some length, he said, "I would like to go back and discuss this with my editor." A couple of weeks later, John and his editor, Grant Salisbury, came to my office to discuss the study. It was October 1963. They indicated that they were going to do something with it.

They began to work on an article and scheduled it for release in late November. Then came the tragic assassination of President Kennedy. The issue in which they were going to introduce *Man, Land and Food* was of course shelved and replaced by one addressing the questions generated by the heartbreaking and abrupt loss of the president. The next few issues, as well, failed to mention the study. I assumed it would never make it into the magazine. Thus I was amazed to see it in the January 6, 1964, issue at the train station. While the study reshaped how we thought about the future, it also jump-started my career.

Man, Land and Food generated a raft of letters, including a highly complimentary one from my thesis adviser at the University of Maryland, Clifford C. Taylor. The letter I treasured most was from Henry A. Wallace, former secretary of agriculture and vice president under Franklin Roosevelt. He congratulated me on the study, discussed the future of technology in expanding agricultural production, and then went on to describe his current project of breeding strawberries on Farvue farm, his home in New York State. In retirement, he had returned to the plant breeding he started with corn in the 1920s that led him to establish the Pioneer Hi-Bred Seed Company and the commercial hybridization of corn in the United States.

When I got back from Wyoming, I was invited to meet with Secretary of Agriculture Orville Freeman, who was intrigued with the report and immensely pleased that a study from his department was getting so much attention. He was also perplexed: He did not know anything about the study because it had never appeared on a plan of work. It was never budgeted. As far as the bureaucracy was concerned, it did not exist.

Above all, Freeman seemed intensely curious about a person

who would individually undertake such a demanding analysis. We hit it off from the beginning and in a short time he created a new position on his staff for me.

Exactly where this experience would take me was not then clear, but one thing was certain: I had discovered in myself a capacity for breaking new ground in thinking about and projecting the future. And I had done it within an interdisciplinary analytical framework, incorporating agronomy, economics, and demography. This systemic approach, a distinctive personal style, would mark every book or article I would ever write. And it would shape each of the two research institutes I would later launch.

2

Early Years:
The Great Depression
and World War II

I was born at home in a small house for hired hands, nine miles west of Bridgeton, New Jersey, on March 28, 1934. My father was a farmhand and my mother, a domestic. After the early death of Grandmom Brown of stomach cancer at age thirty-two, some eighteen years earlier, my father, Calvin—then twelve years old and the oldest of four children—dropped out of fifth grade and left home to work as a live-in farmhand. He sent his meager income home each week to help Grandpop Brown, who was trying to raise the three younger children on his own.

When Pop was fully grown at six feet tall, he was a handsome man, rather English in appearance. His quietness seemed to reflect that of his mother, a Quaker of Scottish descent.

Grandpop Brown was a seasonal farm worker. He and Grandmom and the kids (as soon as they were old enough) worked on farms—picking strawberries and cutting asparagus in the spring, then hoeing and weeding vegetable fields during the summer, picking tomatoes in late summer, husking corn in the fall, and cutting and shocking cornstalks in late fall.

During the winter, Grandpop supported the family by digging ditches. He was skilled in laying underground tile drainage systems. The ones that drain low-lying fields in western Stow Creek Township, where I grew up, are still functioning nearly a century later, including one on our family farm.

My mother, Delia Smith, herself the daughter of a farmer and the fourth of five surviving children, lost her mother to diabetes when she was twenty. Mom, who had dropped out of school in seventh grade, worked as a domestic for a well-to-do family in the nearby hamlet of Hancocks Bridge. About five foot six, Mom was a blonde with a touch of strawberry, which is not surprising given her maternal Irish ancestry. Like Pop, she was a quiet person.

Grandpop Smith accumulated three adjoining farms with marginal soils over a lifetime—not because he ever made much money, but because he never spent much. The son of one of three brothers who migrated from Thüringen, Germany, in 1852 and took up farming in Salem County in southern New Jersey, he was a hardworking, successful farmer. Grandmom Smith was born a Gallaher, as Irish as one could be.

My father apparently met my mother when he was working on the Smith farm. After a short courtship they married in 1933 and moved into the small farmhand house a few miles to the south, just across the border in Cumberland County, where I was born.

As my parents were awaiting my arrival in the early spring of 1934, Pop decided to attempt the jump from farmhand to farmer. He used his meager savings to buy a team of horses and some secondhand farm equipment. After eighteen years of working for a half dozen different farmers, he felt he had to give it a try. Starting to farm in 1934 during the Great Depression, when millions of established farmers were going broke, was a gutsy move—and uphill all the way.

Buying a farm was out of the question, so Pop rented the smallest of the three farms that Grandpop Smith owned. It was partly surrounded by the tidal salt marshes on the southwestern corner of New Jersey, where the Delaware River widens to become the Delaware Bay. We lived not far from Harmersville, a hamlet in the southernmost part of Salem County, near the border with Cumberland County.

The uneven soils, mostly clay in some places and gravelly in others, were not the ones that gave New Jersey its nickname "the Garden State." In addition, the fields were irregular in shape, conforming to the borders of the salt marshes. Mosquitoes were abundant.

The farmhouse was a small wooden structure with a shed, kitchen, living room, and one bedroom upstairs. We had no electricity, no running water or indoor plumbing, and no refrigerator. Mom cooked on a woodstove. The outhouse was about forty paces from the house—but seemed much farther on a cold winter's night! Mom washed our clothes on a washboard in a metal tub. We took our baths in that same tub once a week.

Austerity reigned in our home. We had no music, no radio, and no books. The walls were bare. We never went to a restaurant, never went to the movies, and never celebrated holidays. There are no baby photos of me. The earliest photograph of me is the one in the front of this book, taken the year I started school.

My brother Carl was born on this farm shortly before I turned three. Like me, he was born at home with the local physician, Dr. Carl Ware, in attendance. Out of gratitude for delivering both of us, my parents named my brother after Dr. Ware.

I was named after Lester Cain, my father's favorite cousin, who was a successful dairy farmer.

We lived at the end of a mile-long dirt lane. Mail was delivered to a large rural mailbox located where our lane reached the main road. One Christmas, we discovered in the mailbox a basket filled with an assortment of fresh fruit from an anonymous donor. I still remember the excitement of that moment. We could celebrate Christmas!

Although our living conditions were humble, we always had enough to eat. We had our own garden and produced potatoes and other vegetables. Mom canned tomatoes, peas, lima beans, sweet corn, and fruit—importantly, peaches and strawberries. She made grape jelly and applesauce.

We had a dairy cow and a small flock of chickens to supply eggs and, on rare occasions, a young rooster to eat. Mom baked our bread and we made our own butter and cottage cheese. One of my early household chores was to shake a one-quart jar of cream (not quite full) until the fat globules coalesced into butter. Although it seemed like I had to shake the jar forever, it was only fifteen minutes. Beyond bread and potatoes, we frequently ate a cornmeal porridge, which we called mush, served with milk and molasses. On particularly cold days Mom treated us to "ice cream" by flavoring milk that was partially frozen with some vanilla and sugar.

Muskrat coats were in fashion during the 1920s and 1930s, creating a thriving market for muskrat pelts. For the farmers who owned adjoining marshlands, muskrats were the winter crop. The pelts sold for a dollar each and the carcasses were either sold for a quarter each, given away, or simply discarded. For us, a common winter dinner was fried muskrat and milk gravy—flavored with the remnants of frying the muskrat in lard—served on homemade bread.

Muskrats were so abundant at the time that the women's auxiliary of the township fire company in nearby Hancocks Bridge held an annual muskrat dinner to raise funds. That tradition continues to this day. When I am asked what muskrat tastes like, I explain that muskrat is to rabbit or squirrel as duck is to chicken—much more flavorful.

During the early years spent on this farm, I learned to work. One of my chores as a four-year-old was to clean the horse stables each day. This was particularly onerous because the horse manure and the litter would get wedged between the irregularly sawed planks of the stable floor. I can still remember the frustration!

One of my summertime responsibilities was to keep our field of tomatoes free of Colorado potato beetles. Since the tomato and the potato are first cousins, both members of the Solanaceae family, the Colorado potato beetle thrives on both. We did not have pesticides, so I patrolled the field, carrying in one hand a discarded vegetable can that had an inch of kerosene in the bottom. Row by row, I would walk the tomato field, quickly grab the black-and-yellow striped beetle when I spotted it, and drop it into the can. When I came across a cluster of their bright orange eggs, always laid on the underside of the leaf, I simply squished them with a pinch. Some days I spent hours walking the tomato field to protect it from a pest that, if not controlled, could literally defoliate the tomato plants, destroying the crop.

Herbicides were not yet available and mechanical cultivators did not always get all the weeds, so we also did a lot of hoeing and weeding by hand. Walking through the field, we typically did two rows at a time, pulling the weeds that would compete with the corn, tomatoes, or other crops for sunlight, soil moisture, and nutrients.

Our family did not socialize very much, but sometimes on

a Sunday afternoon we would climb into our 1933 Chevy and visit some of our cousins. Most often we visited the families of my mother's older brother or my father's younger brother, both of whom lived only a few miles away. This was a rare chance for my brother and me to play with other children.

From time to time, Pop would go to the local general store where a handful of farmers gathered in the evening after dinner to talk and tell stories. It was not customary to take children to these gatherings, but for some reason Pop, perhaps sensing my intense interest, took me with him. I sat quietly in the background and absorbed everything. To the extent that I can tell stories, it is an art I learned from these farmers sitting around the cracker barrel.

Somewhere along the way, apparently by the time I was four years old, someone had taught me to read. It was almost certainly Grandpop Smith. I vaguely recall sitting on his knee and doing something with letters. Well before I started school, my father would have me spell for friends and neighbors who would drive down our lane just to drop in and say hello, as neighbors in rural communities did in those days.

My recollection of the first day of school in the nearby village of Canton is simply that there were a lot of people and a lot of noise. I had never seen so many people in one place before. Nearly a hundred students studied in the three-room school. The outhouses were out back, and the cast-iron water pump was beside the school. There was no cafeteria. I enjoyed kindergarten and was thoroughly engaged in learning and finding books to read.

In the spring of 1940, Pop was contacted by the owner of a farm where he had worked several years earlier as a hired hand. The sharecropper was retiring and the owner offered my father the opportunity to sharecrop his eighty-four-acre farm. Sharecropping is an arrangement where the landlord provides the land, buildings, and operating capital while the sharecropper typically provides the equipment and does the actual farming. Income from the sale of crops, milk, and livestock is then shared between the landlord and farmer. Although it was only six miles from where we lived, the soils were much more fertile and the agricultural community was more prosperous. Pop accepted the offer, and in March 1940 we moved.

My new school, Stow Creek School, reflected the community's relative prosperity. It had indoor plumbing and a cafeteria. Upon my arrival, and after the usual testing, they moved me from kindergarten into first grade, making me a year younger than my classmates.

This farm had a dairy barn, which Pop quickly filled with a dozen cows. In addition to selling milk, we also grew a few acres of tomatoes and peppers as cash crops. Here I learned to milk cows, starting with Mollie, an older cow who was gentle and an easy milker.

Pop started farming with a team of horses. Given a choice, he would rather have farmed with horses than with a tractor. When we had only thirty acres of cropland on our first farm, he could manage it with horses. But eighty-four acres was beyond the range of a team of horses, so he reluctantly bought a new tractor, a Farm All A, manufactured by International Harvester.

We were settled away on a good farm and doing well. Then on Sunday, December 7, 1941, the Japanese attacked Pearl Harbor. Suddenly the United States was at war with both Imperial Japan and Nazi Germany. At age thirty-seven, with a family to support and a large farm to operate, Pop was exempt from the draft. But the effects of the war were pervasive. We had air raid drills, where everyone gathered in the school because it was the only large brick building in Stow Creek Township.

As children we looked forward to these drills because

once we were assembled we each got a Popsicle, either a chocolate-covered vanilla pop or an orange-ice-covered one. I usually opted for the latter. At school, we began putting money aside to purchase U.S. savings bonds, saving a quarter at a time, until we filled all seventy-five slots in the savings booklet. Costing $18.75, the bonds could be redeemed in twelve years for $25. Metal became scarce and we recycled everything we could find. Gasoline, tires, and sugar were rationed. Farmers were in a favored rationing category, having special access to gasoline and tires, because producing food was such an essential part of the war effort.

Meanwhile I was enjoying school and reading voraciously. Once class assignments were given, I would rush to finish them so I could read books in the library. This was widely recognized by my teachers come report card time. My fourth-grade teacher, Mrs. Tomlinson, wrote, "His reading and choice of reading material, especially historical books, is outstanding.... The thing he needs to do most is to slow up." The sixth-grade teacher, Mrs. Van Vliet, wrote, "He does his work 'too fast.' This leads to carelessness." This was true, but I was willing to settle for a slightly lower grade because I was learning so much from reading.

During at least one school year, I read over 100 books. I found biographies intensely interesting, including those of our founding fathers. Others I particularly enjoyed were about Abraham Lincoln, Marie Curie, and George Washington Carver. By the time I graduated from eighth grade I had read almost every book in Stow Creek School.

Since we were rather isolated on the farm and since neither of my parents had ever read a book, our dinner table conversations were limited. Biographies opened the world to me in a way that my parents could not. Thus at an early age my sense of self was being influenced by my fascination with these political leaders and scientists. They had addressed the major issues of their time, and I wanted to do the same.

Jim Wood, an older farmer down the road, noticed that whenever we dropped by I would look for their newspapers and then sit quietly reading them while the adults talked. He suggested that each day after school I come by and pick up the two newspapers from the day before—the *Philadelphia Inquirer* and *Bridgeton Evening News*. This quickly became part of my daily routine. Since the newspapers were a bit large for me to hold, I spread them out on the living room floor and read them on my hands and knees. Fascinated by the reports on the war, I followed the North Africa campaign with intense interest. The newspapers used maps to show the advances or retreat of the Allied forces. They showed where Rommel's army was located and described its strategic goals. I learned names of cities like Tripoli, Bizerte, and El Alamein.

Closer to home, one facet of the war was being waged just off the U.S. East Coast. Once at war, we literally had to build thousands of ships, including battleships, destroyers, aircraft carriers, freighters, tankers, and troop transports. Steel for the ships produced at the nearby huge Philadelphia shipyard came from Bethlehem Steel's Sparrows Point Plant near Baltimore. The steel was shipped down the Chesapeake Bay and the Potomac River, into the Atlantic Ocean, up the East Coast into the Delaware Bay, and up the Delaware River to Philadelphia. Unfortunately the United States had little capacity to deal with the German U-boats. Plying the waters off the U.S. coast, they picked off the U.S. ships one by one as they moved between Baltimore and Philadelphia. Although it was not public knowledge at the time, eighty-six U.S. ships were sunk off the East Coast during 1942, many of them along that stretch of coast between the mouths of the Potomac and Delaware rivers.

The response to these attacks was to avoid going out to the

ocean by using the inland canal that connects the upper Chesapeake Bay to the lower Delaware River. Some twenty miles in length, the eastern end of the C & D Canal was only fifteen miles up the river from our farm as the crow flies. Eventually, the U.S. Navy began to thin the ranks of U-boats with much more effective weapons technologies, including destroyers, radar, and depth charges. In 1943, the number of U.S. ships lost off the East Coast dropped to eight.

After nearly two years of the ebb and flow of battle between Allied and Axis forces in North Africa, the Germans and the Italians, who were running out of supplies, were decisively defeated in May 1943. Some 275,000 troops were surrendered to the Allies. Hitler, occupied with mounting problems on the eastern front with Russia, was forced to pull back from North Africa. It was an early turning point in the war.

By this time the air raids on Germany by fleets of U.S. and British bombers, escorted by fighter planes, were rapidly increasing. Then one day the bold headline in the *Philadelphia Inquirer* said 1,000 Allied planes had crossed the English Channel the previous night. We knew then that the tide was starting to turn.

For Christmas in 1943, Emma Dixon, the daughter of our landlord, Theodore Dixon, and a schoolteacher in neighboring Hopewell township, gave me a copy of *Swiss Family Robinson* by Johann David Wyss. When I am asked what book has had the most influence on me, that is the one I cite. What remains with me from that book about a shipwrecked family on an uninhabited tropical island was the father's ingenuity in creating a civilized environment for his wife and four sons in such difficult circumstances.

Our landlord's other daughter, Jessie Lilly, used to pick up Carl and me every Sunday morning to take us to the Cohansey Baptist Church, roughly a mile away in Roadstown. In Sunday school we memorized verses from the Bible. For each verse memorized, we got a small blue ticket, which (surprise) also had a Bible verse on it. If we earned four blue tickets, we could trade them in for a red ticket, and if we accumulated 100 red tickets, we got a new Bible. I saw this as an extraordinary opportunity, a chance to earn something myself. At times I memorized whole sections of the New Testament books, such as Ephesians, Philippians, and Colossians. It did not take long before I presented my Sunday School teacher with 100 red tickets and was awarded a new Bible. Because I was accustomed to working for nothing, getting something in return was exciting, to say the least.

In early 1944, Pop learned of a forty-acre farm for sale in the western end of Stow Creek Township, roughly four miles from where we were living. The owner was asking $2,500. For Pop, the early war period had been years of both good harvests and good prices. He had saved enough money to pay cash for this smaller farm. Mom, however, enjoyed the Dixon farm neighborhood and friends there, and she was reluctant to move. It was one of the few times she demurred when Pop made a decision. The bottom line was we'd have not only a farm but also a home of our own. The soils, though not as uniformly fertile as those on the Dixon farm, were nonetheless quite productive.

This farm, which had electricity but no indoor plumbing, came with seven acres of asparagus. The asparagus beds, which can produce for up to twenty years once established, were aging. But for the first few years on the farm, we cut asparagus beginning in mid-April and continuing through the end of June. The asparagus went to the P.J. Ritter cannery in Bridgeton, New Jersey, roughly ten miles from the farm, for 9¢ a pound. Cutting asparagus is hard, backbreaking work, but there was a good market. We also grew peppers and tomatoes. This farm on Sandwash Road was to become the family homestead, the Brown farm, where our parents spent the rest of their lives. And it was here that our little sister, Marion, was born in 1945. There were nearly three years between me and Carl, and nine years between him and Marion. The farm is still in the family, now owned by my brother and me.

During the summer of 1944, when I was ten, we took our tomatoes to the same P.J. Ritter cannery that processed our asparagus. Much to my astonishment, when we started handing the baskets of tomatoes from the truck to the factory hands, I realized we were handing them to German prisoners of war. They all wore khaki jumpsuits with "PW" hand-stenciled on the back in large, black letters. They were among the troops who had surrendered to Allied forces in North Africa. When given a choice of staying in detention camps in the desert or coming to the United States to work, they chose the latter. With some 600 German soldiers living in our community, the war that I was following so intently in the newspapers suddenly felt very close.

Then in 1945 the war came to an end and the country gradually worked itself back to a more normal existence. Within a few years, Pop had built a barn and again accumulated a dairy herd, this time about twenty cows. Back to milking cows, we divided the milking rather evenly among Pop, Carl, and me. Cows have to be milked twice a day, 365 days a year. And since they had to be fed and milked both before and after school, we were up early each morning and had to milk again after getting home from class.

Our student body at Stow Creek was largely of European extraction with a minority of African Americans and an even smaller minority of Native Americans. The latter were part of the Lenni-Lenape tribe.

In early June of 1947, I graduated from eighth grade, the first in our family to make it through elementary school. Our eighth-grade teacher and the school principal, Henrietta Tomlinson, who had been teaching kindergarten and first grade when I arrived at the school in 1940, took me aside and said that in the evaluation forms that would be submitted to Bridgeton High School, she had done something rare. She had given two students, Jane Fogg and me, straight A evaluations as high school prospects.

A new chapter was about to begin. Bridgeton High School, drawing roughly half of its 1,000 or so students from the town of Bridgeton and half from the surrounding rural communities, was an ethnic melting pot. The diversity from elementary school expanded to include many Japanese Americans whose families had the opportunity of leaving internment camps to come work at Seabrook Farms. We were also joined by displaced Estonians, Latvians, and Lithuanians.

Entering high school meant that we had to make choices about what we wanted to study and whether we wanted to go to college. For someone like me, who was very much engaged in farming, enjoyed agriculture, and was eager to learn more, the choice was simple. On the advice of Mrs. Tomlinson, I enrolled in vocational agriculture on the college-prep track.

For me, high school involved still more travel time on the bus. In addition to spending more time on homework and chores on the farm, I also got involved in sports. In my sophomore year, at age fourteen, I started running cross-country and track. In my junior year I added football, and when the school launched a wrestling team, I immediately became a starter. I fared much better in wrestling, which was organized by weight classes. It was the first sport in which I lettered.

I was on a football squad that was regularly winning championships, but I rarely got on the field. Here size, maturity, and experience were far more important. The coach's philosophy was that if you worked hard and did not skip practices, you were awarded a letter in your senior year. It is the only reason I earned a letter in football.

Although I was doing well in school, I had an underlying feeling of social inadequacy, largely because of my parents' lack of education and the austere conditions in which we lived. With farming taking most of the money, we had little to spend on furniture or clothes. My clothes sometimes drew attention—but for the wrong reasons. It was not until I was in college that Carl replaced our outhouse with an indoor bathroom. Until then I was embarrassed to bring friends home after school.

In addition to classroom study, vocational agriculture students were required to have their own farm projects. If you did not live on a farm, you had to work on a farm to gain firsthand experience with agriculture. In my sophomore year, my project was to build a twelve-by-fourteen-foot coop in which to brood and raise chickens. I was proud of it. The design came from a Connecticut Agricultural Experiment Station pamphlet. My brother and I then started raising broilers in the early months of the year, followed by pheasants in the spring.

One of the things we noticed when we were raising chickens was that whenever you put fresh feed in the feeder or even walked in and stirred up the feed, the chickens, being naturally curious, would come up and eat a bit whether they were hungry or not. My brother and I then set up a schedule so that one of us would feed them first thing in the morning, and again before we went to school. Mom would feed them during the day, and we would feed them when we got home from school, after dinner, and finally just before going to bed. The purpose of the frequent feeding was to get the chickens to eat more and grow faster. We also put vitamin pills in their drinking water. Our strategy worked!

We entered the New Jersey 4-H Chicken of Tomorrow competition, a contest to see who could produce the best chickens in twelve weeks, starting with day-old chicks. At the end of twelve weeks, Carl and I each submitted five birds from our flock for evaluation by the judges. The weight of the five birds entered by other contestants ranged from twelve to twenty pounds. Ours weighed in at twenty-four pounds. Carl's entry won the state competition. He was thirteen years old. The local supplier of the day-old chicks, Garrison's Hatchery, was delighted with the free publicity.

Once the chickens had gone to market, we cleaned out the brooder house and replaced them with pheasants. The day-old pheasant chicks were supplied, free, by the New Jersey Division of Fish and Wildlife. When the chicks were twelve weeks old, the Fish and Wildlife officials would come by with crates and pickup trucks, load up the young pheasants, and release them around the state as part of an effort to rebuild the New Jersey pheasant population. They paid us $1 for each pheasant. Raising pheasants in captivity is not easy, and mortality rates are often high. But we were extraordinarily successful, so we were able to move ahead on a large scale, raising up to 600 at a time.

Early on in pheasant raising, we noticed that some of the birds' legs were splaying, becoming weak and spreading out to the side, making it impossible for them to walk. We learned from our Fish and Wildlife contact that the premixed feed ration for chickens that we were using lacked manganese, an essential nutrient for pheasants. We switched to a premium game bird feed ration that contained a minute but essential amount of manganese, and the affected birds recovered quickly.

On another occasion, some of the pheasants—already several weeks old—started dying mysteriously. We paid Marion, who was only six, a nickel for each dead bird she brought out of the pens. It was much easier for her to walk under the low-hanging wire netting over the pens that kept the pheasants from flying away than for my brother or me to crawl around on our hands and knees. To this day, she likes to remind Carl and me of our child exploitation.

We reported the deaths to the Division of Fish and Wildlife because we had not seen anything like this in the previous batches of pheasants we raised. The officials there were as mystified as we were. But after several necropsies and more research and consultation with game bird pathologists in other states, they identified the cause as eastern equine encephalitis. It turns out this disease is similar to the West Nile virus that was brought into the United States several decades later. Both of these are mosquito-borne, and can be deadly for horses, certain types of birds, and occasionally for people. Just as crows are highly vulnerable to West Nile, pheasants are vulnerable to eastern equine encephalitis. There was no preventative.

With these early projects to work on, some of them before Carl was even in his teens, my brother and I learned about a wide range of issues, including finance and management. We also learned more specialized topics such as building construction, poultry nutrition, and pheasant pathology, to name a few. We were thrilled, motivated, and inspired by the challenge of having our own farm projects. The stage was being set for our first major farming operation: growing tomatoes.

3

Growing Tomatoes

In 1820, Colonel Robert Gibbon Johnson stood on the county courthouse steps in Salem, New Jersey, and ate a tomato in front of an obviously anxious crowd. At the time, it was widely believed that this "love apple," with its passionate red color, was poisonous. To the onlookers' relief, Johnson suffered no ill effects from eating the tomato. Before long, many others were eating tomatoes as well.

Popular though this legend was where I grew up near Salem, the Spanish had long since taken tomatoes from Mexico, where they likely had been brought from Peru, and introduced them into Europe and Asia. Tomatoes were produced and eaten in Spain and Italy in the 1500s. In fact, tomatoes were grown and eaten in Salem's own neighboring Cumberland County as early as 1812. By 1835 they were being produced in large quantities in southern New Jersey. Commercial canning of tomatoes in the area began around 1860.

Cumberland County, where we lived and where I farmed,

soon became the tomato-growing cradle of the country. By the time my brother Carl and I started growing tomatoes, they were one of New Jersey's most popular and most highly valued products. South Jersey supplied fresh tomatoes each summer to Philadelphia and New York. In addition to canning them, the industry turned them into tomato juice, tomato soup, and ketchup. With two tomato processors in Bridgeton, P.J. Ritter and Pritchard's, the summer air was filled with the mouth-watering aroma of ketchup being cooked in huge vats laden with spices. This aroma was an integral part of every summer of my youth.

In addition to tomatoes, other processing crops important to South Jersey included asparagus, lima beans, peas, green beans, and sweet corn. Peach orchards and strawberry fields further added to the mix. It was the farm produce from this area that made New Jersey "the Garden State."

By the spring of 1951, Carl and I were ready to take our farm projects to another level. We planted our first field of tomatoes. It was just six miles from the courthouse steps where Johnson had eaten a tomato in a public display. We leased the land for a year and signed a contract with the P.J. Ritter Company to grow seven acres of tomatoes (28,000 plants) and deliver the produce to the cannery for $32 per ton.

P.J. Ritter provided the tomato seedlings and technical advice through their fieldman, a tomato expert. The seedlings were grown by the company in Cairo, Georgia, and when they reached six inches or so in height they were carefully hand-pulled and put into bunches of fifty each. Their roots were wrapped in damp moss surrounded by brown wrapping paper and tightly wedged into baskets to prevent them from drying out. They were loaded onto a tractor-trailer and driven directly to Bridgeton, where local farmers like us would meet the trailer to get our contracted 20,000, 30,000, or 50,000 tomato plants.

When the truck arrived, we sprang into action. The fields had already been plowed and prepared. Now it was time to plant. At this time, we were still planting tomatoes by hand. Using a tractor-drawn marker to lay out the rows and the cross rows so we would know exactly how far apart to plant the tomatoes, we went to work in earnest.

Once the school day ended Carl and I scrambled to take advantage of the remaining daylight hours. It took us several days to plant all the seedlings. Then it was time to cultivate to control the weeds and to keep an eye out for insects. Later in the season, we'd be checking for diseases such as the tomato blight.

During our first few years of tomato farming, we, like almost everyone else in the area, grew the Rutgers tomato, a variety that dominated the production of tomatoes for processing in the northeastern United States for a generation. A highly productive, tasty tomato that was released by the university in 1934, it had been developed by Lyman Schermerhorn, a professor of plant science at Rutgers University, and his graduate students.

But this era was soon to end. In the early 1950s the Campbell Soup Company, which had a large tomato-processing plant in Camden, was also investing heavily in developing new, more productive varieties of tomatoes. Before this initiative, the Phi Beta Kappa of tomato growing was the "Ten Ton Tomato Club." Any farmer who harvested ten tons or more of tomatoes per acre was automatically a member. Within a few years, it became the Twenty Ton Club. It was an impressive example of what the systematic application of science to agriculture could do.

Of all the crops that we could grow, Carl and I chose tomatoes. Why? For one thing, the growing season of the tomato meshed well with the academic year. That is not to say there was no overlap, because the tomato fields had to be planted in April or, at the latest, early May—well before school was out. At the other end of the season, when school started in the fall, there were still tomatoes in the field. This too was scramble time for us.

At the same time, tomatoes are fun to grow. They are so responsive and productive. Displaying its fruit—some ripe, some ripening, and some still green—a tomato plant is a work of art. And I like the distinctive aroma of a tomato plant. To this day when I see a tomato plant I cannot resist smelling it.

One of the challenges for us was how to finance our ever-expanding tomato operation. My brother and I had an understanding with Pop. As long as we did our chores and got everything done and done well, Pop did not care what we did with the rest of our time. So in the spring, for example, my brother assumed the responsibility of milking not only the cows he was responsible for, but also mine. I, meanwhile, would run a mile and a half to a local farm to spend a couple of hours before school helping the farmer cut his four acres of asparagus. He paid $1 an hour, enabling us to accumulate some cash. It also provided some training, since I was running the mile on the school's track team.

In addition to picking strawberries and cutting asparagus for other farmers, we would also help at hay baling time using an old truck we had bought to haul hay bales from the field to the haymow quickly. Farmers liked to hire Carl and me because we worked so hard. We also competed with each other. I was the first to pick 100 baskets of tomatoes (thirty-five pounds each) in one day. Then Carl took it to 102. After that, the record went back and forth between us: 105, 107, 108, and then 110. It was no accident that I won the Cumberland County

Junior Tomato Picking Championship in 1949! Nor that Carl was selected as a New Jersey Star Farmer by the Future Farmers of America!

In 1949 we bought our first tractor—a J.I. Case two-plow, mid-sized tractor of ancient vintage—largely with earnings from picking tomatoes for other farmers. At 10¢ a basket for picking tomatoes, it took 2,000 baskets to pay for the tractor.

In late August 1951, on the weekend before I was to report to Rutgers University for freshman orientation, we faced a logistical problem. While I had a driver's license, Carl did not. Once I left for Rutgers, Carl would still need to get tomatoes from our farm to the cannery a dozen or so miles away. The problem wasn't so much the lack of a license, really, because young people on a farm often drove locally before they were licensed. The problem was that Carl had never driven a truck laden with tomatoes stacked five baskets high.

With this in mind, we decided to take a load to the cannery on Saturday, the day before I left. Loading over 200 baskets of tomatoes onto a truck is an art in itself. The body of a tomato truck is designed so the tomato baskets can be stacked in an extended pyramid, stretching from the front to the back. The sideboards enabled us to put another layer of baskets leaning in against the pyramid on both sides to stabilize it. It was a tried-and-true way of moving tomatoes from the farm to the processing plant. Our aging 1935 Chevrolet truck carried at least four tons of tomatoes.

We decided that Carl would drive the truck to the cannery and I would follow in the pickup soon after. He would have to get it in line, because there was always a long line of trucks waiting for hours to be unloaded.

The last stretch of road of five miles or so to the cannery was straight. Carl driving the heavily loaded truck came up behind a local farmer who was drawing two or three implements behind his tractor. Carl prepared to pass and was already well onto the left side of the road when he realized the farmer was going to move out into the center of the road to make a right-hand turn into his driveway. The truck's wheels went over onto the dirt shoulder and the truck began to lean with its heavy load. Carl pulled it back onto the road, but not all the tomatoes made it back with him. Part of the load tumbled off, leaving tomatoes strewn several inches deep across a swath of the road. He pulled over to assess the damage and wait for me.

By the time I arrived, cars had already driven over the road—and through the tomatoes. But as though they were driving through newly fallen snow, the drivers had kept to one lane, carefully using the same ruts to minimize the damage.

Someone suggested we call our field agent at P.J. Ritter. We called from the farmer's house and the agent arrived quickly. Taking stock of the situation, he saw that most of the tomatoes on the road were still in good condition. Many were bruised and some were cracked, but it was obvious we had picked them carefully and that they were of unusually high quality. He suggested that we borrow a couple of shovels or scoops from the farmer to get as many of the tomatoes back on the truck as we could, preferably without sand or gravel. He said we wouldn't be able to get all of them, but we could get most of them.

He requested that we then ask the farmer if we could park the truck behind his barn, out of public view, since these cracked tomatoes could become a public relations issue for Ritter. And he told us to bring the truck into the plant the next morning at 5:30 a.m., when they would unload it immediately to minimize the chance of the cracked tomatoes spoiling.

Despite the loss of a small part of this load, we delivered many other loads and did well that year. We were officially tomato farmers. And since we did most of the work ourselves, much of the check that we got in November for all the tomatoes we had delivered put us in a position to buy another tractor—a brand-new one. My brother and I knew exactly what we wanted, a new Ford two-plow tractor. I suggested that he go ahead and buy it. Carl had worked hard and I wanted him to have the experience and satisfaction of buying the tractor.

He went to the local farm equipment dealer, who obviously knew us, but who was not well prepared to sell to a fourteen-year-old. It took him awhile to realize that my brother was serious and that he wanted not only a tractor but also the plow and cultivators to go with it. We bought that tractor in the fall of 1951 for $2,100 with an initial down payment of $700 and the remainder to be paid in $700 installments in the fall of each of the next two years, a typical arrangement for farmers.

We had started growing tomatoes just when the industry was on the verge of rapid change. After a couple of years of planting by hand, we got a mechanical transplanter. The transplanter, on which four people could ride, planting two rows of tomatoes at a time, was drawn behind the tractor. Mounted on each side of the tractor hood were two drums filled with water that contained a liquid fertilizer. Thus, as each plant was going into the ground, roughly half a cup of water would be released at the same time to provide moisture around the roots of the plant as well as the essential nutrients: nitrogen, phosphate, and potassium. This helped to get plants off to a faster start than with traditional hand-planting.

As our tomato-growing operation grew, we shifted from the local tomato processor, P.J. Ritter, to Campbell Soup, which could readily handle our larger harvests. It is hard to believe today that we were producing and delivering tomatoes to the Campbell Soup plant in Camden, New Jersey, for $34 a ton. Today you can carry $34 worth of fresh tomatoes home from a supermarket in a shopping bag!

During our first year of tomato growing with only seven

acres, Carl and I picked nearly all the tomatoes ourselves. But as I expanded the acreage, eventually to seventy acres (280,000 plants) in 1958, we needed a lot of help with the picking. Our pickers included classmates, friends, and, as we grew larger, seasonal workers from nearby Salem and even some from Puerto Rico via a contract with the Puerto Rico Department of Labor.

Our sister, Marion, though she was much younger, also became part of our operation. By the time she was eight years old she was driving the tractor for the wagon that provided pickers with empty baskets. As she drove the tractor slowly across the field, carefully following a row so as not to damage tomatoes, we unloaded small stacks of empty baskets in the field so they would be in place for the tomato pickers. This is not the only thing Marion did in our tomato growing operation, but it was the part that she liked best.

Many years were to pass before mechanized tomato pickers took to the field and plant breeders began breeding tomatoes that were tough, designed to withstand the mechanics of picking and the stresses of being handled and shipped long distances. The luscious, flavorful tomatoes I had grown up with would soon be limited to a few garden varieties. Today the once widely grown Rutgers tomato has been replaced by another Rutgers product, the Ramapo tomato, grown by gardeners throughout the northeastern United States.

Carl and I have always had a close, understanding relationship. We took pride in the things that we had accomplished together from an early age. But while I enjoyed school, Carl did not. Carl dropped out of high school during his junior year and worked as a plumber's apprentice during the winter. Once he became a licensed plumber, he set up his own business and turned his share of the tomato operation over to me. His entrepreneurial skills then took a different form. Using his knowledge about various houses from plumbing assignments, he began identifying those that looked dilapidated from the outside but were in fact structurally sound and in good condition inside. He bought these underpriced homes and then renovated and rented them. He now owns some thirty-five homes.

In February 1958, as I was thinking about the prospect of eventually settling down as a tomato grower in southern New Jersey, I realized that I might never get to the West Coast to see California. Given that I had a couple of weeks clear, I decided to hitchhike to a suburb of Los Angeles to visit Gloria D'Eve Ward, a woman who was in the group I went to India with and who was then teaching high school in Inglewood. I had $37 of traveling money. Carl drove me to the southern end of the New Jersey turnpike, less than twenty miles from home. From there, I hitchhiked north, connecting with the Pennsylvania turnpike and crossing Pennsylvania, Ohio, and into Indiana before leaving the turnpike and heading southwest. From Indiana, I hitchhiked across southern Illinois, Missouri, and into Oklahoma.

In Oklahoma, I was picked up by a professor from the University of Pittsburgh who was en route to a new teaching assignment in northern California. He was driving a large Buick that was several years old. He was pleased to have someone with whom to share the driving, which meant we would not have to stop anywhere overnight. As we left Oklahoma, crossed the Texas panhandle, and went into New Mexico, the car began to overheat because he had antifreeze in the radiator, not surprising since he was from Pittsburgh. He was not eager to stop. I suggested that we turn the heater up full blast and open the windows. The heater in a car of that era functioned in a sense as an auxiliary radiator. This technique worked and we continued across New Mexico and Arizona into southern California. When he was ready to head north, he dropped me off in Pasadena, not far from where Gloria lived.

I spent a week with Gloria. We visited Disneyland, the Rose

Bowl, and local historic sights. Then I headed back, taking more or less the same route. The only time I was stalled was at midnight that first day. I found myself stranded on the road for a few hours in Needles, California, a sparsely populated area in the Mojave Desert on the Arizona border. Eventually I got a ride and made it back to New Jersey three days later.

Despite the occasional lulls, my hitchhiking times were surprisingly consistent. It took sixty-nine hours going out and seventy-two hours coming back. One of the great things about hitchhiking is that it is inexpensive. When I got back to New Jersey, I still had much of the $37 that I had left with. Even though I was a successful tomato grower, money was still scarce. In establishing the price for contract-grown tomatoes, the companies always seemed to have the upper hand— negotiating low prices that would nonetheless provide all the tomatoes they needed.

A little hitch in my plans came in late spring of 1958 when, like all able-bodied males at the time, I was subject to two years of compulsory military service. I was ordered by the U.S. Army to report for a physical. In mid-summer of 1958, I was ordered to report for active duty. When word got out that I would soon be going into the army, the farm equipment dealer, to whom I still owed money, called the fertilizer dealer, whose fertilizer supply to us was to be paid for in the fall after the tomato harvest. They called the chairman of the local draft board, arguing that it would be economically catastrophic for them and for the community if I were to leave for the army. Since both dealers were influential community leaders, the draft board chairman exempted me from duty. And, in fact, that year I marketed 1.5 million pounds of tomatoes, becoming one of the largest tomato growers in New Jersey.

The eight-year tomato-growing period of my life, 1951 through 1958, began during my senior year in high school, spanned the four years at Rutgers (see Chapter 4), the months I lived in villages in India in 1956 (see Chapter 5), and two years beyond that. I had developed an attachment to the land. Even now whenever I return to Stow Creek for family visits, driving through the countryside with its fertile sandy loam fields, patches of woodland, and creeks, I enjoy a sense of peacefulness and of being grounded. But by late summer 1958 the challenge of growing ever-more tomatoes was not as attractive as it once was.

To begin with, for farmers who did not own their own farm, the economics were not promising. You could make a living by renting land on a year-to-year basis, as I was doing, but only barely so. Land available for renting was usually inherently less fertile. And since you were renting year-to-year, you could not, for example, set up a soil-building crop rotation. Beyond that, as a result of having lived in India, I was beginning to develop an interest in the growing imbalance between food and people in the world and wanted to do something about it. Based on all these considerations, I decided that what I really wanted to do was to join the Foreign Agricultural Service (FAS) of the U.S. Department of Agriculture. This would take advantage of my training and experience in agriculture while giving me the chance to work abroad.

But before we get to the FAS, I need to tell you about two exceptional experiences that helped shape my thinking, and indeed my life.

4

Ag Science at Rutgers

It was mid-July 1951, and I was driving north from the farm toward Rutgers, the State University of New Jersey, in my red '36 Dodge pickup along with Dorothy Harris, my girlfriend at the time. Dot, a very pleasant dark-haired girl, who later went on to nursing school, was part of the small group of young people in our rural community.

At Rutgers, where I had been accepted some months earlier, I was scheduled to see Dean of Students Howard Crosby to discuss tuition, which was due at registration. My principal income came from growing tomatoes, but the cannery did not pay for the tomatoes until well after the end of the season, usually in November. I needed to see if they could wait until then for the payment.

As I sat in front of Dean Crosby's desk, he asked me to repeat my name. He then began leafing through a four-inch-thick, three-ring binder until he came to my name. He asked, "You're from Cumberland County, right?" I said yes. He said, "You have a four-year full tuition scholarship."

A weight fell from my shoulders. Some months before, I had gotten a letter from the county superintendent of schools, Roland Mulford, saying that I had been nominated for a state scholarship. I had read the letter with interest, but hearing nothing more, I thought little of it. But here I was with a four-year scholarship, one that I had not even applied for. For a farm boy with meager resources, this was like manna from heaven, a gift from the gods.

Selecting a college had been easy. I wanted to study agriculture, and Rutgers—the land grant university of New Jersey—had an outstanding College of Agriculture. It also offered a major in General Agricultural Science—exactly what I needed as a farmer. The only college to which I applied, it was just 120 miles from the farm, close enough that I could commute on weekends, and more often when needed, to continue farming while in school.

The College of Agriculture offered a rich fare of science courses, leaving me feeling like the proverbial kid in a candy store. A number of basic science courses were required for an agricultural science degree, but many other options were available. Among the courses I feasted on were biology, bacteriology, chemistry, organic chemistry, physics, geology, soils, soil physics, genetics, meteorology, climatology, entomology, animal physiology, plant physiology, plant pathology, and more practical courses like plant propagation, animal nutrition, weed control, agricultural engineering, and agricultural economics. And, since Rutgers was a land grant college, it also was the base of the New Jersey Agricultural Experiment Station. This meant that many of our faculty members were actively engaged in cutting-edge applied research.

The opportunity to major in general agricultural science rather than in a more specific field such as botany, soil science, or animal husbandry played to my innate desire to see issues in the broadest possible light. It also led me to integrate ideas across fields of knowledge. At a time when there were no majors in environmental science, a major in general agricultural science was about as close as a person could get.

Because of its sterling reputation for science offerings, the College of Agriculture appealed to many premed students as well. To say that Rutgers' soil science department was outstanding is an understatement. In 1943, Albert Schatz, a graduate student, discovered streptomycin in heavily manured farmyard soil outside the Rutgers plant pathology building and college stables. He was twenty-three years old, one of several graduate students working with Professor Selman Waksman. The team discovered eighteen antibiotics including streptomycin, actinomycin, and neomycin, which we know commercially as Neosporin.

In 1952 Waksman was awarded the Nobel Prize in Physiology or Medicine. In the summer of 1954, the new Institute of Microbiology opened at a large, freshly constructed building on the Rutgers campus funded largely with streptomycin and neomycin royalties. The discovery of streptomycin and the many other antibiotics that followed at the Rutgers College of Agriculture fundamentally altered the practice of medicine worldwide.

Part of the required curriculum at the ag school was a one-year course in public speaking. Taught by Richard Reager, author of the then-popular college textbook *You Can Talk Well*, it was the single most useful course I had at Rutgers. Completing it did not automatically make one a great speaker, but it did provide a grounding in the basic principles of effective public speaking. I learned how to engage an audience, to speak from notes rather than reading a prepared text, and to focus a talk on a goal.

I could not have known then that one day I would earn millions of dollars in speaking fees. The first time I got a $50,000 speaking fee, I could not resist comparing it with picking tomatoes at 10¢ a basket. To earn as much by picking tomatoes, a person would have to pick a half-million baskets—more than anyone could do in a lifetime. The investment in education has paid handsomely, though I never keep the speaking fees for myself.

Another required course was in technical composition, a course designed mostly for researchers on how to structure an article and how to write clearly when dealing with complex technical issues. It, too, would come in handy. My term paper was entitled "The Economic Importance of the Earthworm."

These courses in communication, both oral and written, played to my deep desire to communicate complex issues to people in terms they could understand.

Some people aspire from an early age to be a writer. I never did—and I still don't—but if you want to share your research findings, your "ideas," with large numbers of people, you have no choice but to write. So here I am, a reluctant writer, with shelves filled with my own books.

Rutgers was hard work, but I had time for some play. One of my early acquaintances on campus was Tom Price from Long Branch, New Jersey. Early in our freshman year, while we were out walking after dinner, we came across a Volkswagen Beetle. Since it was such a novelty car, we wondered if we could lift the rear end off the ground. When we discovered that we could, we thought it would be fun to place one wheel on the curb. It was! Tom, being an inch or two taller and about twenty-five pounds heavier, was exceptionally strong, as the world would soon learn.

In January 1952, as a freshman, Tom tried out for crew and made the team. Shortly thereafter Coach Logg teamed him with his own son, Chuck Logg Jr., who was a senior, so the two could compete in the pairs event in the U.S. Olympic trials. Chuck and Tom won that competition, earning the right to represent the United States in the 1952 Olympics in Helsinki. There they won the gold medal.

Tom's ascent through the rowing ranks was extraordinary. He began rowing in January and he and Chuck won their Olympic gold in July. In six months, he had gone from novice to world champion! The keys to the U.S. team's victory were Chuck's experience and Tom's power.

My closest friend at Rutgers was Larry Suydam, also an aggie. We had a number of classes together, including one in bacteriology with a good-natured professor, Herbert Metzger. Each week we had an afternoon lab experiment that required a written report. One week we decided to do a report together but each of us would claim it as our own. We signed it LES. Larry, whose name was Lawrence Earl Suydam, claimed the paper was his because those were his initials. I claimed it was mine because it was the short version of my first name. Professor Metzger understood very well what was going on, but he couldn't figure out how to resolve the issue. Finally he graded the paper and simply gave each of us the same grade. But we knew we could get away with this only once.

In 1958, Larry moved his keen interest, enthusiasm, and sense of humor from North to South Jersey, to become associate manager of my tomato-growing operation. We are lifelong friends.

The economics of getting an education at Rutgers worked

out well. Not only did Rutgers offer a full-tuition scholarship, but the College of Agriculture, under the widely admired leadership of Dean Frank Helyar, had also created housing opportunities for needy students. During the Depression, Dean Helyar had taken an inventory of the entire 170-acre College of Agriculture campus, looking for nooks and crannies that were not actually used for anything, searching for places where students could live. The Phelps House, an old farmhouse on the west side of the campus that had come with one of the college's land acquisitions, comfortably housed twelve students. Another, where I lived, was "the Towers," an unused area atop the entomology building. This space, where the walls were mostly glass, may once have been a greenhouse. It housed eleven of us.

One attraction of these group living arrangements was that we had our own kitchen and dining area. We contributed a modest fee to cover food costs. Each student would take a turn doing the shopping and preparing dinner for a week, which meant we only had to shop and cook one or two weeks a semester and we got to enjoy everyone's home cooking. The tendency was for each person to prepare his mother's favorite dishes. While our meals were never lavish, and cooking skills varied, we actually ate rather well. Dinner was a time for sharing ideas and experiences, a break before evening study.

One of the more illustrious members of our group was Jim Davis, the end on the Rutgers football team. In those days, players did not specialize in offense or defense. They played both. I was intrigued with Jim as an outstanding athlete. And since he had grown up in the city, he was fascinated by my farm background and tomato-growing operation.

In exchange for these living arrangements on the college farm, we each had some campus responsibility. In my case, it was to open the college library from 7 to 9 p.m. two nights a week. It was an ideal job. Because few books were checked out and there were not many visitors in the evening, it was a great place to work on my own class assignments.

One Sunday afternoon on the farm during my sophomore year at Rutgers, as I was packing my bag to head back to school and preparing to say good-bye, Pop pulled from his pocket a $10 bill and offered it to me to help with school. This came as a complete surprise because we had never talked about the folks helping me through college. They could barely make ends meet, so helping me at college was not something I'd ever even thought about. I can't remember whether or not I accepted the $10. I hope I did because it would have made Pop feel good.

At Rutgers, I learned some things about myself. One was that while I excelled at things that I wanted to do, I did poorly at things I did not want to do! In my freshman year, algebra was a required course. I had difficulty seeing the value of algebra in growing tomatoes. So I devoted little time to studying it, rationalizing that since I scored high on math aptitude tests I could somehow be sharp enough when the final exam came to make it through the course. But when the postcard arrived at the end of the first semester, I had received an F in algebra. I had to take the course again.

Algebra aside, my overall academic record merited nomination for membership in Alpha Zeta, the oldest national agricultural honor society. Among the various qualifying steps was to write a scientific paper on an assigned topic. Mine was to investigate "Some Effects of Para-chlorophenoxyacetic acid on the Parthenocarpic Set of Tomato Fruit."

In high school, I had been able to do sports, to farm, and to still maintain a decent academic record. I could not do that in college with the heavy courseload, a part-time job, and the commuting between the campus and the farm during the tomato season. Sports had to go. Although I did well on the freshman cross-country and track teams, it became clear that I could not afford the training time needed.

In a recent conversation, Larry Suydam reminded me that on a weekend in our sophomore year he accompanied me to Bridgeton to help with the plowing. We arrived Friday night and rose early on Saturday morning to start plowing the fields I had rented. We took turns on the tractor, plowing all day Saturday, all night Saturday, and all day Sunday before heading back to campus. Such was life when combining school and farming! In fact, sometimes weekends would not be enough to get all the farming done and I would have to miss classes for a day or two.

Social life was restricted both by time and resources, with dating limited largely to hometown girls on weekends. The girl I dated throughout this period was Harriett Pennington, who went on to become a radiologist. A group of us living on the college farm organized a square dance demonstration group, the Rutgers Promenaders. Led by Karl Reinhardt, a housemate and square dance caller, we performed at various events. Today, fifty-nine years later, the Promenaders are still going strong.

Though time was scarce, I did participate in the university's intramural wrestling tournament, a competition for wrestling teams from the many fraternities on campus and other living groups. In my sophomore year, our college farm group entered a team. I helped to organize and coach the College Farm Wrestlers. We did well but did not win the tournament. In our junior year, we were much stronger—and we walked away with the title. After losing to one of us, a fraternity team wrestler was overheard saying, "Those farmers are strong."

In our senior year, we totally dominated the tournament,

putting a wrestler in the finals in virtually every weight class. Ironically, I was the only member of the college farm team who had actually wrestled before—which is why, by default, I became the coach. Fortunately, intramural competition required only a rudimentary mastery of basic wrestling skills to fare well. A little organization and a focused effort went a long way. Our two championship trophies were proudly displayed in the ag college library.

Early in my senior year, I realized that by the end of the first semester I would satisfy the requirements for graduation. This opened the attractive option of taking a package of agricultural education courses that included a six-week stretch of practice teaching. It was my good fortune to be assigned to Woodstown High School, a progressive rural school, roughly forty minutes from the farm, for the practice stint. Teaching agriculture was attractive not only because I enjoyed it but also because if I ever suffered a physical injury while farming, teaching could be my fallback career.

As we were coming down the homestretch in our senior year, we had to start making a set of decisions about what to do next. At about this time, we were asked whether we wanted our diplomas to read "Bachelor of Science" or "Bachelor of Science in Agriculture." The overwhelming majority of students opted for the plain BS because they thought it would give them access to a broader range of job opportunities. But a handful of us, including me, wanted to be identified as agricultural scientists. We wanted to be known as aggies. It was a matter of pride.

As we approached graduation, many of my classmates began interviewing for jobs with various agribusiness firms, the New Jersey Department of Agriculture, or the New Jersey Division of Fish and Wildlife. Since I might be offered a job that I would find attractive, I did not plant tomatoes that year. But when the time came, I could not bring myself to interview for jobs. Growing tomatoes was what I really wanted to do.

After graduation in the spring of 1955, without tomatoes to look after that season, I accepted a job as a truck driver for Seabrook Farms, a large food-growing and processing company that was near home and, among other things, was one of the pioneers in freezing vegetables. As we moved into the fall, it was time to harvest spinach. The truck followed the spinach cutter through the field. The mechanically cut spinach went up an escalator and dropped into the truck, which resembled a dump truck, except that its body was much larger. The trick, of course, was always to keep the truck in the right position so the spinach would fall into the truck and not onto the ground. That was the defining skill of the job.

At the end of the year, perhaps influenced by my truck driving skills, Seabrook Farms offered me a position as an assistant manager of the Salem/Woodstown division, a 3,200-acre spread of vegetables. Sweet corn, lima beans, peas, and spinach were among the principal crops. The manager was Gene Taylor, a classmate and friend from Rutgers. The entire operation was highly mechanized. We had a staff of perhaps eight or ten tractor drivers and equipment operators, plus mechanics whose job it was to keep the equipment going all the time. Sometimes we worked around the clock in shifts to get the lima beans planted or the peas harvested on time. Overall, it was a well-organized, scientifically advanced operation.

I began in this new position on January 1, 1956. This phase of my career was to be short-lived, however. Kathleen Hoffmeyer (now Petri), one of the four women in our agriculture college class and a friend for several years, had been filling in for our Cumberland County 4-H Club agent, Kenneth Picket, while he was on sabbatical. When she learned that she could nominate a local candidate for the International Farm Youth Exchange program, which was managed by the National 4-H Club Foundation, she proposed me. A few months later I learned that I had been selected as one of ten U.S. farmers, all recent college graduates, to go to India and live with village families.

5

Life in the Villages of India

Some of the books I read while growing up were about Americans traveling abroad. Prominent among these were Richard Halliburton's books on travel, which were high-drama experiences as he climbed mountains, trekked across deserts, or swam the Panama Canal. Another book that stood out was by Osa Johnson, who, along with her husband Martin, was an explorer and adventurer. Her book, *I Married Adventure*, about life in Africa and the South Seas, also fueled my interest in traveling. Now I would be journeying to the far side of the planet to live in villages in India. I couldn't wait.

At this time transoceanic travel was in the process of shifting from ocean liners to airplanes, although it was still the era of prop planes, low speeds, and short flights. Our group of seventeen young farmers—headed for India, Nepal, and Pakistan—traveled by ship from New York to Bombay (now Mumbai) via the Mediterranean Sea and the Suez Canal.

The months between notification of my selection for the

International Farm Youth Exchange (IFYE) and the beginning of orientation were short ones. I continued working at Seabrook Farms until the time of departure to give them ample time to find a replacement. I had also contracted with P.J. Ritter to grow fifteen acres of tomatoes.

Even though Carl and I were no longer partners, when I left for this six-month commitment, he readily took over the tomato operation for me in late summer, managing the harvest.

At the end of July 1956, I took my first plane ride, flying from Philadelphia to Ames, Iowa, for an intense week of orientation at Iowa State University with 175 IFYE exchangees there from thirty-six countries. The IFYE was a cultural exchange program between the United States and some forty other countries. Co-sponsored by the U.S. Department of Agriculture (USDA), the Ford Foundation, and the local and state Extension Services, it was one of many exchanges that evolved after World War II to promote better understanding among countries. There were many briefings and much discussion on how to adjust to life in another culture, particularly one as different from our own as that of India.

Among those attending this weeklong gathering were Indian, Pakistani, and Nepalese delegates to the United States, which allowed us to meet our exchange counterparts who were now living with U.S. farm families. The timing of these farm exchanges was shaped by the seasons. The best time to be in the United States, of course, is spring through fall. For those of us going to the subcontinent, it was better to arrive in September after the monsoon season.

Once we completed the week in Ames, our group headed to Washington, DC, for an additional week of orientation. As I thought about the plane trip to Washington, it occurred to me that I could hitchhike and save the money that otherwise would be spent on airfare. With most of my personal resources invested in the tomato crop yet to be harvested, every dollar counted. Another member of our group, Earl Drane from Mississippi, also found the idea appealing, so we hitchhiked back to DC together.

We left Ames at about 9 p.m., after our final day of orientation. The first substantial ride was on a flatbed tractor-trailer hauling barrels of buttermilk north to Chicago. Since the cab would only comfortably hold one of us and the trailer was not fully loaded, I volunteered to ride on the back with the buttermilk. Within a few hours, as we were approaching Chicago, the driver let us off so we could pick up the turnpike heading east. At the service center where we'd been dropped, by now 2 a.m. or so, I saw a car with Pennsylvania license plates and a man asleep in it. I suggested to Earl that we wake him up and volunteer to help with the driving. Although he was a bit groggy, it did not take long for him to agree. And since he lived in southeastern Pennsylvania, we would end up close to Washington.

With our orientation complete, we sailed from New York to Bombay, leaving New York on a Greek ship, the *Queen Frederica*, on August 17, 1956. As we left New York, we found ourselves being escorted by Hurricane Betsy, tossed and turned by the huge waves crashing on deck. For two days we were caught in the storm's path, moving with it in a northeasterly direction across the Atlantic. At one point the wind speed measured on the bridge hit 120 miles per hour!

The ship pitched and tossed so much that even many of the ship's veteran crew became seasick. For some reason, it did not bother me at all. On the second day of the storm, I was one of only four passengers who showed up for breakfast. But then as the day went on our path and that of Hurricane Betsy separated, and the rest of our transatlantic crossing went smoothly.

The time on the ship was not all our own. We all had to study Hindi, Urdu, or Nepali—depending on our host country—

amidst the many activities to distract us, such as a Scrabble tournament that I organized. And the food was exceptional.

Seven days after leaving New York, we sailed through the Straits of Gibraltar into the Mediterranean where the water was smooth and blue and the temperature was rising. We made a quick stop in Malaga, Spain, to pick up water, fresh food, and other supplies. From there we sailed eastward to Naples, Italy, where we disembarked to change ships and continue our journey to Bombay.

A five-day layover in Naples gave us a chance to visit nearby Pompeii. Several of us also took the train to Rome, spending a couple of intense days there visiting St. Peter's Basilica, the Colosseum, the Roman Forum, and other sights. For young American farmers, some of whose grandparents were homesteaders, this exposure to ancient Europe was eye-opening.

Back in Naples, we boarded the SS *Victoria*, an Italian liner destined for Singapore. As we approached the Suez Canal, we learned that we had arrived in the early stages of a northward flow of ships. We would be at anchor for a couple of days. Enterprising tourism firms were on hand to take passengers from ships at anchor to Cairo for two days of sightseeing and then to the southern end of the Canal to reunite with each person's ship.

Most of us had barely been out of our hometowns. We saw the usual tourist sights, like the Pyramids, but experienced so much more. This was a civilization that had functioned continuously for several thousand years. Taking a trip on a small boat on the Nile one evening in the moonlight was revealing. We learned that the downriver traffic is carried by the steady flow of the Nile, but because the onshore breezes move in the opposite direction, raising the sail on small boats provides the energy to travel upstream. My guess is that this river transport system, powered entirely by natural forces moving both downstream and upstream, played a central role in both the emergence and longevity of this early civilization.

We had not been told by the captain of the *Victoria* that when our ship emerged from the southern end of the Suez Canal into the Red Sea it would not be able to stop for the tourist boat because of the many ships following close behind it. This meant we would have the unexpected thrill of reboarding the *Victoria* while it was moving. Our motor launch pulled up beside the ship, and the crew lowered a stairway that we climbed to get back on board.

As we left the Red Sea and headed eastward, we made a stop at Aden, a port that was then part of a British protectorate, later to become Yemen. Walking around the city, we saw poverty that was more acute than any of us had ever before witnessed. It was an early exposure to what we would later see in some parts of India. From there we were eastward bound again, sailing across the mouth of the Persian Gulf and then along the coasts of Iran and Pakistan. We put in at Karachi, where our five delegates for Pakistan disembarked. We would not see them for several months. The rest of us, ten headed for India and two for Nepal, continued on.

Once in Bombay, twenty-seven days after we had pulled anchor in New York, we were met by the agricultural consular officer, Roy Sellers, and IFYE's director in India, Mr. Raisinghani (a graduate of University of California–Los Angeles), who welcomed us to India and briefed us on agricultural issues. Two days later we headed for New Delhi on an Indian airline DC-3. When we landed we saw a host of photographers, reporters, and newsreel cameramen. We assumed there must be a celebrity aboard the plane. But they were there for us! At that time, there were not many Americans in India. It was just the beginning of a very warm reception by the people of India. For a time, it seemed that every American official in Delhi, as well as many of the Indian officials, expected us to attend either a tea or dinner with them.

In New Delhi, we had yet another week of orientation, this one with briefings from Indian government officials on what we could expect in the villages and how to deal with various cultural issues that might come up, including those associated with diet, dress, language, and religion. During that week, I learned that India would be holding the finals to select its wrestling team for the 1956 Olympic Games to be held in Melbourne. Another member of our group, Ward Armstrong, a graduate of Oregon State University, was also a wrestler. Together, we convinced the other members of our group that we should attend this event.

Because there were so few foreigners in India, we were given ringside seats. In between matches, we talked with Indian officials about wrestling generally and about collegiate wrestling in the United States. The officials hit upon the idea of having Ward and me give an exhibition of American collegiate wrestling, once their team had been selected. Since neither Ward nor I had wrestling gear, we borrowed wrestling tights from the Indian wrestlers. The crowd enjoyed it, seemingly as fascinated with our match as we were with the selection of their team.

To our surprise, the next morning's newspapers covered not only the selection of the team, announcing who would be going to Melbourne in each weight class, but they also carried a piece on the match between two American collegiate wrestlers. One of the consequences of the extensive news coverage was that as I traveled to various villages in India, I was sometimes challenged by the local wrestlers. Indeed, in the first village, Pardi, located in central India on the Deccan plateau about fifty miles from Nagpur, I faced my first challenger.

The local wrestling champion, Mongol, a friendly guy who

smiled a lot, was ready when I arrived. The villagers organized a match that would take place not on mats, as is customary with American wrestling, but in a wrestling pit, a shallow depression filled with loose sand to cushion falls. It became a major social event, with villagers coming from miles around. Villagers placed bets amid a buzz of discussion and anticipation.

In trying to assess my prospects, I considered the usual things: experience, quickness, balance, conditioning, and strength. With quickness and balance, it appeared to me likely to be a draw. With conditioning, the advantage was clearly with Mongol because I had been traveling for several weeks, including a good part of the time onboard a ship where there were no workout facilities. With experience, it seemed to me that I had a strong advantage, and since I was at least fifteen pounds heavier, I also had the edge in strength. Mongol's big advantage was that we were wrestling in a physical environment, a sandpit, that was familiar to him. It took a while for me to get used to moving around in the sand. Mongol also had the hometown support, but I had a feeling that at least my host family was hoping that I would come out on top, so to speak.

When the match began, we were both somewhat cautious, each trying to get a feel for the other before attempting a takedown. A missed takedown can leave one vulnerable. Mongol wrestled well, but as the match progressed my experience became the decisive factor. Even though we could not communicate directly, we both enjoyed competing and interacting with each other. And I was pleased because it provided a connection with the villagers, another way we could relate to each other.

My host family in Pardi had eight children, seven girls and one boy. The boy, Joe (short for Jawaharlal), had been to the States under the IFYE program and was my age. One sister was a couple of years older. One was away at secondary school. The other five ranged from ages four to thirteen. All spoke English.

My host father, who owned the largest tract of land in the village, was also the village head. An exceptional farmer, he had won a national rice growing championship and was awarded a new Ford two-plow tractor—identical to the one my brother and I had bought just a few years earlier. In a village that had been totally dependent on bullock power for tillage, my being able to teach them how to use the tractor elevated my standing.

Being part of a large family was fun. At night, the younger girls would use their school slates to teach me such things as my numbers in Marathi. I learned to count from one to ten—and still can. *Ek, daon, tin, chaar, panch, sha, sat, aath, nuu, dha.*

A couple of times during my three weeks in this village, I visited the local school. The students were delighted when I participated in their games. Youngsters always like to compete with adults, and it was great fun for them to watch me try to master the intricacies of their games.

At one point in my stay, I was helping to dig a major irrigation canal, working in my usual energetic way. A farmer, one of the many from neighboring villages who were helping with the digging, was apparently impressed by my work habits and, through my host father, suggested that his daughter was available for marriage. To sweeten the deal, he offered to include two rice paddies. I had not, of course, seen his daughter, nor was I likely to anytime soon, given the nature of arranged marriages. I tactfully pointed out that I had commitments for many months into the future and therefore would have to decline his generous offer.

During my stay in Pardi, my hosts, who were largely vegetarian, began to wonder if I was getting enough protein, so my host father asked the local shukari (hunter) to see if he could find a wild boar for us to eat. The next day, he and another villager came bearing a boar weighing some 125 pounds that he had shot in the nearby hills. Carrying the pig with its front and back feet tied together and suspended on a pole, they dropped it—literally—at my feet. Now what? Fortunately, in my youth I had observed a few hog killings on the farm, where two or three families would get together to slaughter and process two, three, or four hogs. Although at the time I was too young to be actively involved, I did acquire a sense of how to butcher a pig.

So we went to work. My host family and I dressed the pig, then proceeded to carve it into various pieces—hams, shoulders, ribs, etc. One of the things I was concerned about was trichinosis, a pig-borne disease we had learned about in one of my courses at Rutgers. I had no idea whether that disease might exist here so I made sure the meat was cooked thoroughly before it was eaten. Some of my family members ate the pork along with me. It was quite tasty.

What was revealing, though, was that after we had eaten a few meals of the choice cuts, and because there was no refrigeration or other ways to preserve the meat, my host father strung all the remaining pieces on a clothesline well off the ground where dogs could not reach them. I was mystified, but the meat was left there overnight. To my surprise when we arose the next morning, it was all gone. Many of the villagers, though they were by habit vegetarians, would eat meat if it were available.

Soon I had to say good-bye to my home away from home. With sadness I waved from the rear of a bullock cart to my Indian father, mother, brother, and sisters, who had treated me as their own.

Then I traveled by train to the southern tip of India, where I lived in a village near Trivandrum. Located in the state of Kerala, this was tropical India at its finest. It is also the state in India that has the largest Christian population. Here I was treated as a guest of the village rather than of a particular family, so I never developed close personal ties as I had with my host family in Pardi. Much of my time was spent traveling about the region, observing the local agriculture, which was dominated by rice and coconut production. It was here that I learned how to transplant rice seedlings from the nursery into the water-covered fields, a technique imported from Japan.

During my visit in Kerala, I began to sense that I was not getting to see the real poverty in the country. An English-speaking Indian friend and I decided one day to go out for lunch on our own. The plan was to visit homes unannounced at lunchtime and see what would happen. In the first five homes we visited, there was no food for a noonday meal.

On the sixth attempt, we learned that they had just finished their meal but had saved part of the food for their evening meal. They offered this food to us. The meal consisted of boiled tapioca root flavored with a meager amount of chili sauce. With no eating utensils, we both ate from the one container with our fingers. The tapioca root, although not particularly tasty, was filling. They then asked us to stay for coffee. While waiting for the pot to heat, we noticed that the man of the house had disappeared. He returned shortly after with a cup and a glass borrowed from a neighbor. When we said goodbye to this hospitable family, we generously reimbursed them for our lunch.

There were no windows in these homes, only open doorways. The houses had earthen floors. They had no tables, chairs, or cupboards. Everyone sat and slept on the floor. Their stove consisted of three large rocks arranged to support the cooking pot. The typical family in this area cooked their meal in the evening and then ate the remaining portion for breakfast and, as we witnessed, there was no lunch.

From here I went to the other extreme in the extremes that

are India. Traveling by train, I headed north to stay with the Rajah of Mankapur in a small community in northern India, not far from the border with Nepal. My host, Rajah Raghocucha Pratab Singh, was an affable, interesting man. He had two children, both of whom were away at school. His wife had died some years before. He was in his mid forties, a good six feet tall, slightly bald, and somewhat overweight.

The Rajah's palace grounds covered eight acres. He had fifty servants. At mealtime, he had me sit at the head of the table. Five servants stood at attention around the table, anticipating our needs. If I picked up a piece of bread, a servant would insist on buttering it for me.

In the morning, the wake-up call came in the form of a tea tray delivered to my room. Even getting dressed in the morning became something of a challenge, unaccustomed as I was to being dressed by a pair of insistent servants who hadn't the least understanding of English.

When traveling with the Rajah, I was surprised at the respect accorded him by the peasants. With few exceptions, when His Highness approached, the villagers would stop whatever they were doing, clap their hands together, and bow reverently.

Although the territory once controlled by the Rajahs and Maharajahs of India had been taken from them in 1947 when modern India was created, they had retained the palaces in which they lived, a small area of surrounding land, and payments from the government that would support them throughout their lifetimes. Interestingly, when the local people needed grain they still came to the Rajah and he would give them handouts. It was an established system, one that he was honoring even though he no longer controlled the vast lands that he once did.

While we were there, he offered to take me on a photo safari in the Terai, the foothills of the Himalayas that lie along the

India-Nepal border. Whenever we traveled locally, we had the choice of using his elephant or the Buick. For the safari, the elephant was the obvious choice.

Two things I remember about riding his large elephant: One, you are quite high off the ground. And, two, as the elephant walked there was a gentle rolling motion not unlike that on a ship. Aside from an occasional deer, we did not spot any other large mammals. What we did see were women from nearby villages headed for home with firewood tied into a bundle and balanced on their heads.

While living here I decided this would be a great chance to see Nepal, which was about 100 miles from the Rajah's palace. The Rajah's nephew, who was about my age, and I traveled as far as we could by train, then proceeded by bicycle, and then by foot.

One of the striking things then about the Nepalese country-side, virtually all of which is mountainous, is that there were no roads and therefore no wheels. Along the narrow mountain trail we were hiking into the country, we saw many Nepalese on their way to India carrying bundles of hides, baskets of fruit, and bags of rice. Those going back home to Nepal were bearing large containers of kerosene. As we moved further into the country, we saw both hill ponies and water buffalo used for transport.

Three things I remember about the Nepalese: They were a trim, wiry population. Many of them had Mongolian features. And they had an unusually high incidence of goiter, as could be seen from their enlarged thyroid glands. In this mountainous country, there was little iodine in the diet, and the iodized salt that we take for granted was not widely available.

All in all, I was treated exceptionally well by the Indian people at all levels, whether they were host families or government officials. Living in Indian villages was a rare experience for a young American, a sentiment that was shared by every member of our group. Because my three hosts were in north, central, and southernmost India, I studied a geographical cross-section of agriculture from intense rice cultivation in the south to the wheat-growing regions of the north. These months would change forever how I viewed the world.

One of the things I did while in India was to write a column for my hometown newspaper, *The Bridgeton Evening News*. Sending back periodic reports, though not usually newspaper columns, was expected of all IFYEs. While staying with the Rajah, I had a chance to reflect on my experiences in India and to catch up on my columns.

Getting home from India was not quite as simple as getting there. The Arab-Israeli war that broke out in October 1956 led to the sinking of many ships in the Suez Canal, which meant our return tickets by ship to Europe were useless. Our sponsors back in Washington booked us flights instead. In New Delhi, we boarded a TWA Super Constellation to head to Europe. On hand to see us off at 2:30 a.m. were a large group of Indian friends and some Indian IFYE delegates whom we had met in Iowa.

Daybreak found us over the desolate and barren desert of the Arabian peninsula. We made our first stop at Dahran, an Arabian town and U.S. Army base for refueling. Midmorning found us setting down in Basra, Iraq, for breakfast. Then, to avoid the Middle East trouble spots, we flew a northern route over the mountainous, snow-covered terrain of Turkey. In Athens, Greece, our next stop, near-freezing temperatures provided a chilly contrast to the weather we had just left behind. From Athens, it was on to Rome, and then to London.

Because flying was so much faster than sailing, we arrived in Europe nearly three weeks before our ship, the SS *United States*, was due to sail from Southampton to New York. With all this time to spend in Europe, we broke into smaller groups. Tom Trail from the University of Idaho, a delegate to Nepal, and I decided to travel together. Leaving London, we crossed the channel by ferry to Belgium, where our first stop was at a Brussels youth hostel. After a day in Brussels, we headed for the land of dikes and windmills.

Then we started to hitchhike. We had addresses of some Europeans who had been in the States under the IFYE program. At one point as we were hitchhiking southward on the German autobahn, we flagged down some NATO trucks operated by Germans that were moving in our direction. We asked them, in English, if we could get a ride, and they said no because the rules forbid picking up hitchhikers. We pointed out that as American taxpayers, we were helping finance their operation, indeed, helping to pay their salaries. After an extended discussion they yielded and gave us a long lift toward our destination.

While on the continent, we visited a family living in an alpine village in Switzerland. The daughter, earlier an IFYE to the United States, took us on a tour of a Swiss dairy farm. She also arranged for a personal tour of a watch factory where we saw the internationally famous watches being assembled.

Then it was on to Paris, where a French agricultural student, Gerard de Campeau, took us on a two-day tour of the city. The day before Christmas we left with him for northern France to spend the holiday with his family at their country estate near Lille. Like the Swiss scenery, French food was the best we had come across in our travels. Then it was back across the Channel to London and south to Southampton to rejoin our group and catch the SS *United States* to New York. This time with Tom cemented what was to become a lifelong friendship.

Upon returning to the States, one of our responsibilities as IFYEs was to give talks, preferably with slides, on life in our host countries. My talk was entitled simply, "Life in the Villages of India." I gave dozens of talks to service clubs, such as Rotary and Kiwanis, and to farm and church groups throughout southern New Jersey. Having learned the principles of public speaking from Professor Reager, I now had the chance to test them on audiences.

One of the things that I often did to involve an audience was to demonstrate how saris are worn. Most people know the sari is simply a strip of cloth, about ten by three feet, which is wrapped initially around the waist, tucked in, and then draped diagonally over one shoulder, hanging down the back. I often asked for a volunteer, preferably an attractive young woman, who would come up on stage to be my demonstration model. When I was giving a talk in early January 1959 to a group of IFYE delegates just returned from India about how to use slides in their own talks about life abroad, I selected Shirley Woolington to help me demonstrate. An attractive, personable blonde with a ready laugh from a Wyoming ranching family, she caught my attention . . . and soon my heart.

After each talk, Mom would collect the sari and carefully wash and iron it. Although her understanding of my travels in India was limited, she wanted to support what I was doing. Whenever I headed out for a talk, the sari was always ready.

Living in India had been a fascinating experience, but I did not expect that it would influence what I would do with my life. When I left for India I was growing tomatoes and planned to do so for the rest of my life. But a couple of years after returning, I realized that was not enough. While in India, I had become sensitized to population pressure. Although India only had 416 million people when I was there, it seemed densely populated even then. I was concerned about rapid population growth and how it frustrated efforts to eliminate hunger and malnutrition and thus the opportunity for children to fully develop both physically and mentally.

By the late summer of 1958, I had decided to apply for a position with the Foreign Agricultural Service (FAS) of the USDA to work on international agricultural issues. This was an obvious place to begin because I had gotten to know the agricultural attachés in New Delhi. When I contacted the FAS personnel office, they informed me that a degree in agricultural economics was required. Analyzing world commodity prices, trends, and markets depended on a working command of economics.

I then applied, belatedly, to the agricultural economics department at the University of Maryland and was accepted. Soon I was rooming at the university with fellow IFYE Tom Trail, who was working on a master's degree in agricultural education.

Once September began, I was spending money, not earning it, and I decided to delay paying off a modest bank loan that I had used to help finance the tomato crop. The banker was trying to contact me through Pop, who relayed the message to me the next time I was back on the farm over a weekend. I stopped at the banker's house the following time I was up for a weekend visit, but when I got there he was out to dinner. I left a message with his fifteen-year-old son, which may or may not have been relayed to his father. I had wanted to assure him that I fully intended to pay off the loan.

The next thing I knew the bank sent a notice to the farm saying that foreclosure proceedings were underway and that the bank would be selling my farm equipment, which I had offered as collateral for the loan, at a public auction. By the time I learned of this, it was too late to intervene. This was embarrassing and so unnecessary, since I would have sold the tractors and equipment to repay the loan. And worst of all, I lost the chicken house that I had built as a fourteen-year-old. It was a classic case of having too many balls in the air and dropping one.

This loss was a low point in my life. I was disappointed with myself. The weakness in my planning was that I had not anticipated that joining the FAS would require a degree in agricultural economics. Thus the big challenge was to try to squeeze all the courses required for a master's degree and a dissertation into nine months from September through May before I ran out of money. I spent the first semester catching up with the other graduate students who had studied economics as undergrads. During the second semester, the challenge was to complete the course requirements and to write and defend the dissertation.

The administrative folks in the agricultural economics department—not anticipating that someone would complete a master's degree in just two semesters—had not ordered a diploma for me. So I could not technically graduate until the summer school graduation. But with the degree requirements satisfied, I was hired by the FAS, reporting to work on June 1, 1959, in the Asia branch.

Meanwhile, during the one-week spring break in the second semester I had driven to Wyoming to see Shirley to try to convince her to come east to work so we could spend more time together. Some months later, she took a job in Princess Anne, a rustic, small town on Maryland's eastern shore, as an assistant agricultural county agent. This enabled us to spend weekends together. By early 1960, we had decided to marry. We were married in the All Souls Unitarian Church in downtown Washington, DC, by Reverend James Reeb, someone we both admired for his human rights work. Like Shirley, he was from Wyoming. Sadly, a few years later when he was marching for civil rights in Selma, Alabama, he was struck in the back of the head with a club and died.

In 1960, we spent Thanksgiving in New Jersey on the farm. Shirley was in an advanced state of pregnancy when she tripped and fell as we were walking through a cornfield. Neither of us thought much about it, but on Monday shortly after we returned to Princess Anne and Washington, respectively, I got a phone call early in the morning from Shirley saying that we now had a son. He had arrived six weeks ahead of schedule, but he weighed in at a healthy six pounds. I promptly boarded a bus from Washington to Princess Anne.

After checking on Shirley to make sure she was doing well, I went to the nursery to see Brian, our son! I had high hopes for him, although even my wildest dreams did not include his one day becoming a world-class kayaker.

Then we had to get practical. Since Brian had arrived early we were missing some essentials, so I did all of the baby shopping: bottles, diapers, a bassinet, the works. Shirley's plan to work through the end of December was no longer an option. We bundled everything up and headed back to the Washington area, where we found an attractive basement apartment in Takoma Park, Maryland, our home for the next few years.

6

Monsoon Failure in India

Sometimes our lives are shaped by specific events. For me, one of these came in the fall of 1965—nine years after my life-changing six months in India. The U.S. Agency for International Development (AID) mission in New Delhi asked the U.S. Department of Agriculture (USDA) for someone to help them evaluate an early draft of the agricultural section of India's next five-year plan. Secretary of Agriculture Orville Freeman, with whom I was working as foreign policy advisor, decided that I would be the one to do it.

Almost immediately after I arrived in New Delhi and started reviewing the plan, something else caught my attention: the condition of that year's grain crop. The officially estimated grain demand for 1965 was 95 million tons, but I soon began to wonder whether a harvest anywhere near this amount would materialize. Reading several newspapers each morning, as I routinely do—in this case, the *Times of India*, the *Hindu*, the *Indian Express*, and the *Hindustan Times*—I found reports of drought in virtually every corner of the country. Although this climatically diverse country is always experiencing both droughts and floods somewhere, in 1965 drought appeared to be almost everywhere.

Other random bits of information reinforced my concern about the projected harvest. At a reception one evening shortly after I arrived, I met the head of Indian operations for Esso (now ExxonMobil). When I casually asked him how business was, he said it was great—diesel sales to fuel irrigation pumps were nearly double the previous year's because farmers were pumping continuously to try to save their crops. Also, an embassy staff person I wanted to meet while in New Delhi had said he would be on vacation, but it turned out he was actually there when I arrived. An avid duck hunter, he usually took off a few weeks in the fall to go hunting on a lake up north, but this year he canceled his vacation because the lake was dry.

Furthermore, an agronomist working with AID traveled extensively in rural India and often stopped his car in the countryside to take soil samples, a hobby of his. But he complained to me that he could no longer get good core samples: the soil was so dry it crumbled and fell out of his auger as he withdrew it. This was something that I had never seen in my years of farming.

After pondering these and other incidents, and compiling information from newspaper stories on crop damage in various districts and states as reported by local officials, I became convinced that India faced a huge crop shortfall. And since the United States was the dominant world grain supplier—the only country that could even think about filling a deficit of this scale—this warranted an urgent cable to alert Secretary Freeman. It was already early November, and the logistical challenge of moving massive quantities of grain with little warning and preparation could be overwhelming. With a potential deficit of the magnitude that was in prospect, the secretary needed the information as soon as possible simply because of the time it would take to get wheat from grain elevators in Kansas to ports in New Orleans and Galveston. If we got adequate quantities to the ports, grain could be loaded quickly onto ships in case we had to mount a massive food-relief effort.

If I were going to sound such an alarm, it would be necessary to estimate the size of the deficit, despite having only fragmentary data. If my estimate was too high, the United States would overmobilize and waste resources. But an estimate that was too low could lead to famine. I worked to strike the right tone in the cable to Freeman. Written in cablese, it read:

> After week study have concluded crop will be much less than officially admitted. Believe poor crop will result in major food crisis, perhaps most serious in recent history.
>
> Crop shortfalls not localized. Poor monsoon nationwide, affecting nearly every state. Private conversation with Food Secretary Dias last evening confirms gravity of situation.
>
> In light above fast developing situation suggest evaluate our position considering stock levels, possible use grain sorghum supplement wheat and merit using Indian ports full capacity to get much food as possible in country now before crisis reaches its worst.
>
> Estimate 10–15 million tons or more grain imports from all sources may be needed to sustain India's 480 million until next major harvest.

With a copy of the proposed cable in hand, I went to the embassy control officer on a Saturday morning, only to learn the cable would have to be officially approved and thus would have to wait until Monday at the earliest. No cable left the embassy that was not approved by Ambassador Chester Bowles or someone acting on his behalf.

The unorthodoxy of what I was trying to do dawned on me. Although I was not a member of the embassy staff, I was making an estimate of the grain deficit that the embassy should be making, and I was trying to use embassy communications facilities to send a message that no one knew about or had approved.

Later I learned that on Monday morning the staff had debated whether this cable, which contrasted strongly with anything the embassy had reported, should actually go. After all, I had not been asked to assess the harvest. It was not an official part of my mission. From what I have since learned about that meeting, John Lewis, the AID mission director, argued that if the cable did not go through official channels, he was certain that I would send it to Freeman via private channels. Therefore, he said it was better that it go through the embassy. He won the argument—the cable went as drafted, but with a P.S. in bold type at the bottom: "Country team preparing separate message on food situation."

The cable actually went to Washington on Wednesday, November 10. On Friday of the following week, I received a cable from Secretary Freeman. It was short and cryptic: "Please meet me in Rome tomorrow morning." He would be in Rome attending the weeklong biennial conference of agricultural ministers organized by the U.N. Food and Agriculture Organization.

At that point, I asked to meet with India's minister of food and agriculture, C. Subramaniam, a friend and someone I respected, to share my assessment with him. I urged him not to play it down when he got to Rome, unless he was convinced that it was off base, because it would slow things down and the needed grain shipments might not arrive in time. He agreed because he too was beginning to sense the potential magnitude of the deficit even though he did not mention any specific number.

Then I had a second request. Since I was to meet Freeman in Rome the next morning, I needed a seat on the Air India flight leaving for Rome that evening. The airline had said the flight was full. Minister Subramaniam arranged for me to be on the plane.

When I met Secretary Freeman on Saturday morning, he said he had shared my cable with President Lyndon Johnson (LBJ). My analysis played to one of LBJ's deepest concerns: that India was neglecting its agriculture as it concentrated on industrialization and was assuming that the United States would fill any grain deficits that might result. If India continued on this path, it would become dangerously dependent on the United States in the event of any crop shortfalls, at a time when scores of other countries also depended on U.S. grain.

LBJ knew that if the recent agricultural trends in India continued, eventually India's grain needs would exceed the United States' capacity to meet them. It was carrying only very limited grain stocks that could serve as a cushion in the event of a crop shortfall. When an Indian official was asked by a reporter about the adequacy of the country's grain stocks, he responded, "Our reserves are in the grain elevators in Kansas."

It was this casual thinking about food security in India, a country with a population more than double that of the United States' and growing by 10 million per year, that alarmed the president and led to what came to be known as the "short-tether policy" on U.S. food aid. LBJ had asked Freeman to get a commitment from the Indians to develop their agriculture—and fast. Any continuing food aid from the United States would be contingent on this. By giving this assignment to the secretary of agriculture, without informing the State Department,

LBJ was signaling his lack of confidence in the State Department, or at least in Ambassador Bowles, a Kennedy appointee who was reputedly "soft on the Indians." This was why I was so abruptly called to Rome.

India was facing a potentially massive famine. I wanted to make sure that both governments understood the gravity and urgency of the situation. Rarely have two governments been in a situation where the stakes, measured in human lives, were so high.

The meeting between Freeman and Subramaniam actually stretched into several meetings. They were held at a private location: the residence of the U.S. ambassador to Italy, Frederick Reinhardt. The goal was to keep the meetings secret and away from the watchful and perhaps already curious eyes of the press.

Freeman, Subramaniam, and I met on Monday morning to discuss the situation. They asked me to draft an agreement between the two countries based on our discussion. At the end of the day, I had a draft. It was distributed to both Freeman and Subramaniam for their review as a basis for discussion the next morning. This daily ritual of discussion and rewriting continued for three days. The agreement was short, three pages double-spaced.

I knew what India had to do. The government's food price policy, which catered to the urban population by imposing ceiling prices on wheat and rice, had to be replaced with a floor price guarantee for the farmers growing these grains. If farmers were to invest in irrigation pumps, fertilizer, and land improvements, they had to know that at harvest time they could get a price for their crops that would at least cover costs.

Fertilizer supplies had to increase rapidly. This meant shifting fertilizer production from the public sector to the private sector. It was taking on average nine years to build fertilizer plants in the public sector—a profoundly laggard performance that was leading to fertilizer shortages.

I also knew that the high-yielding dwarf varieties of wheat, initially developed in Mexico by Norman Borlaug and his colleagues with support of the Rockefeller Foundation, had been tested in India and had performed very well. India needed to accelerate the dissemination of these high-yielding wheats, which would produce twice as much as traditional varieties with a given amount of land and water. To short-circuit the time-consuming process of multiplying seed in test plots over a number of years, we suggested that the Indian government import a shipload or two of wheat directly from Mexico to get seed to farmers quickly.

Once we had negotiated the agreement that contained these essential points, Freeman cabled a draft to LBJ for approval. The president approved it immediately, and Secretary Freeman signed the agreement, in essence committing the United States to providing massive food assistance as long as India adopted the reforms. Although my original invitation from the embassy was to critique the agricultural part of India's forthcoming five-year plan, I was now actually writing a new agricultural plan for India—one that the embassy did not yet know about.

There were differences. The Indian government's agricultural plan was a much longer, detailed bureaucratic document. My new draft was only a few pages on the key initiatives needed, but its strength was that it linked the movement of wheat from the United States to the implementation of a new food production strategy in India. The monsoon failure and the massive looming grain deficit had changed everything.

Subramaniam could not sign this without Prime Minister Lal Bahadur Shastri's consent. Freeman asked that I return to New Delhi and convene a meeting with Chester Bowles and

John Lewis, explaining to them their responsibilities in implementing this agreement, assuming that either Shastri or Subramaniam signed it on behalf of India.

There was one small wrinkle. When I arrived at the airport in Rome on Friday night, TransWorld Airlines (TWA) would not let me board the flight to New Delhi because I did not have a visa. The original visa for India was good for one visit only. Fortunately for me, Indira Gandhi, who was minister of information and broadcasting at the time, was also visiting Italy to accept an award. She had attended a small dinner for Secretary Freeman hosted by the Indian ambassador to Italy on Tuesday night in which I was included. Having had that brief contact with her at the dinner table, I decided to approach her and her entourage as they were preparing to board the same flight. I explained the situation and asked if she could intervene on my behalf and get me on the flight. She did and TWA let me board.

My assignment on returning to New Delhi was intimidating. At the time I was thirty-one years old—just seven years off the farm and feeling self-conscious about convening a meeting with the U.S. ambassador and the AID mission director. Ambassador Bowles, a formidable figure, had served presidents Roosevelt, Truman, Kennedy, and now Johnson. In addition to serving in the critical position of heading the Office of Price Administration during World War II, he had served Connecticut both as governor and congressman. After serving as under secretary of state to Dean Rusk in 1961 under Kennedy, he had returned to India as ambassador for the second time, having served previously during the late Truman years. And John Lewis, the AID mission director, was a widely respected development economist. There was no reason for me to think this meeting would be easy.

John Lewis was calm and relaxed, and Bowles was civil, but

he scarcely contained his resentment over being bypassed in the negotiations. I got to the point quickly as I explained the reason for my quick trip to Rome a week earlier. After describing our week of negotiations, I pulled from my inside jacket pocket a copy of the agreement approved by LBJ and signed by Freeman. Bowles would not even be a signatory to the agreement.

The meeting was short. What made the situation manageable for me was the knowledge that LBJ himself had initiated the meeting in Rome and had specifically requested the agreement that we negotiated with Subramaniam. Bowles and Lewis were obviously not happy with this and it was not the most cordial of meetings. Then I had to wait for India's response and get the document signed by either Prime Minister Shastri or Minister Subramaniam. At least that was my hope.

Subramaniam was in a difficult situation. He obviously could not talk about an agreement he had reached with the Americans while under duress, but he handled the situation with great skill. He included all the key points that were in the agreement in his proposed new plan for Indian agriculture. In effect, he said: Our agriculture is in trouble. We could be facing a huge grain deficit, a potentially massive loss of life. We have to reform our agriculture. Here is what we need to do.

He was a popular political figure and an effective member of the Indian Cabinet. He said he would resign if his plan were not adopted. After two cabinet meetings, and despite strong resistance from the finance minister, he got his new plan for Indian agriculture approved. He then signed the agreement, which I carried back to Washington.

One thing the Indians did not anticipate was the extent to which LBJ was going to use food aid—his short-tether policy—to force the Indian government to follow through on every measure in the agreement. We had a sense of the timing when certain measures had to be accomplished. If they were not, the ships would stop leaving U.S. ports. It took the Indians a while to realize that LBJ was dead serious about the reforms. Several times in the months ahead, the ships stopped sailing because India had not fulfilled its part in implementing the agreement. They would move again only when India had met its commitments. U.S. Under Secretary of Agriculture John Schnittker, with whom I worked closely, was centrally involved in managing the short tether.

The greatest challenge was actually importing the 10 million tons of grain in a single year when India previously had never imported anywhere near this amount before. To assess whether—and how—this massive amount could be moved in time, the secretary called on logistics specialists in the USDA, men who had served in the Army Quartermaster Corps in World War II. During the war they had become masters of moving equipment and arms from point A to point B. Their ingenuity was boundless.

What they did to greatly increase India's port capacity was to lease one of the largest supertankers afloat at the time, the *Manhattan*. They then anchored the massive ship, which was longer than a football field, in the Bay of Bengal and used it as a port. On one side, ships from the United States arrived with grain that was pumped on board and then unloaded on the other side into small, flat-bottomed, local boats called *dhows*, which were about thirty feet long. Thousands of *dhows* were used to move the grain up the Ganges River and its tributaries to reach the parts of the country where the drought was most severe and the risk of starvation the greatest. It was remarkably successful.

Another innovation was to dedicate certain trains within the United States to load up at the grain elevators in Kansas, Oklahoma, and Texas, and transport the wheat directly to the ports in Galveston and New Orleans. As soon as their cars were unloaded, the trains would turn around and, as Orville Freeman put it, "hightail it back to reload again." In that way, we were able to move the wheat into export position very quickly. During the next year, the United States, working closely with the government of India, moved 10 million tons of wheat from the Great Plains of the United States to the cities and villages of India, halfway around the world.

Final data on the 1965 Indian harvest showed it coming in at 77 million tons of grain—18 million tons below the Indian government's original estimated consumption. In the effort to stave off famine, the United States that year shipped a fifth of its wheat harvest to India. At that time, it was the largest movement of food ever between two countries. Some 600 ships, nearly two a day, left U.S. ports laden with wheat for India. Measured by the number of ships used in a single logistical operation it ranks high on the all-time list. This record flow of food from the United States to India avoided what could have been one of history's most devastating famines.

The situation in late 1965 was one where I knew exactly what had to be done. There was no question in my mind. There was an enormous backlog of agricultural technology that could be brought into play in India to help eradicate hunger and stave off the threat of future famine. At that time, I noted that the new technologies could not solve the food problem—they would only buy time with which to slow population growth.

With the new agricultural development strategy, India doubled its wheat harvest in seven years, a record for growth in production of a food staple in a major country. No country, not even the United States, had ever managed such rapid growth.

For the United States, this was one of our finest moments. And not just because millions of lives were saved, but because

LBJ saw a rare opportunity to restructure India's agriculture by dramatically boosting land productivity. My responsibility was simply to identify and incorporate into the agreement the measures needed to transform Indian agriculture into a thriving, fast-developing farm sector. For this fledgling public servant, it was a heady experience.

In the meeting with Subramaniam just prior to going to Rome, I had pointed out that the history of Indian agriculture showed a tendency for monsoon failures to cluster. When a monsoon failed, there was a well-above-average chance that the next one would also fail.

With this in mind, Walt Rostow, then chairman of the Policy Planning Council at the State Department, decided we should convene a conference of aid-donor countries to brief them on the progress in our massive food-relief effort with India and also to discuss the prospects for the 1966 harvest. The two-day conference was scheduled for April 4–5, 1966, in Paris. I was asked to kick off the conference on the morning of the first day with an overview of the situation and close it with a wrap-up at the end of the second day.

On the home front, Shirley was pregnant with our second child. We weren't worried about the timing, because the baby was scheduled to arrive during the last week of March, right around my birthday on March 28. But that date came and went and we kept counting. And, finally, although the baby had not yet arrived, I had to get on the plane for Paris. Then I could only hope that the baby would not come until I returned three days later.

I gave a rousing opening talk, emphasizing not only the issue of food but also that of population—the importance of family planning and ultimately of population stabilization. That night the embassy control officer relayed a cable to my hotel room: "A girl. 7 pounds 6 ounces. All is well. Shirley." Now my record was 0 for 2. Sadly, I had missed the birth of Brian and now Brenda.

It was decided that I would catch a plane back the next day, but since the plane was not to leave Paris until late morning, I could give a preliminary summary of the conference and a renewed call for action first thing in the morning. The reason for rescheduling my talk was announced. I then informed the conferees that Brenda was our second and would be our last child; the children were five years apart. This, I said, was family planning.

As the 1966 monsoon got underway, Rostow called to see if I had any sense of how it was proceeding. Fortunately I had arranged to get a rainfall report by cable from the embassy in New Delhi every Friday. With their data, I was making by hand a color map showing cumulative rainfall state by state. I sent the latest one of these to Rostow so he could get a visual sense of how things were looking. Big mistake! He then wanted me to do a colored map for him every week from then on.

Not surprisingly, the 1966 monsoon was also a weak one. Again, it took several million tons of U.S. grain to fill the gap. But this time the effort proceeded much more smoothly. The reforms were being implemented on schedule, and we had worked out the logistics of moving massive quantities of grain into India.

One of the hallmarks of the USDA during the Kennedy-Johnson era, the eight-year span when Freeman was secretary of agriculture, was the department's growing involvement in international agricultural development. In 1964 the USDA, working with the AID, had created a new agency—the International Agricultural Development Service (IADS). Matthew Drosdoff, an agronomist who had been the Food and Agricultural Officer for the AID in Vietnam since 1962, became the first agency head. In contrast to the Foreign Agricultural Service, whose responsibility was to develop markets for U.S. farm products, the purpose of the IADS was to help develop agriculture in third-world countries. In many countries the AID subcontracted the agricultural part of their program to the IADS.

In 1966, it was decided that the agency should be playing more of a policy role, and Secretary Freeman appointed me IADS administrator. I had no idea this was coming, but I was both pleased and honored.

Two years earlier the agency had been cobbled together very quickly, with personnel donated from other agencies in the USDA. Unfortunately, this meant that the various agencies often sent employees who were about to retire and not their most productive. To help make it a more effective agency, I hired some talented young staffers from outside the department, including I. M. Destler (who got his master's in public administration from Princeton), William Abbott (a White House fellow who had edited the *Harvard Law Review*), and William Jones, editor of *Development Digest*. From within the department, I hired Lyle Schertz and Dana Dalrymple.

As the youngest agency head in government, I needed to learn a lot quickly. To help me, I recruited the experienced Mollie Iler from the embassy in Rome, the one who had typed each draft of our agreement with India, as my administrative assistant. One of the advantages we had, whether in setting up a project or implementing it, was that we could draw on the vast pool of skilled professionals in the sixteen agencies in the USDA, such as foresters from the Forest Service, agronomists from the Soil Conservation Service, plant breeders from the Agricultural Research Service, and professionals from over a dozen other agencies.

We had a huge range of on-the-ground projects going in thirty-nine countries, including expanding rice production in Senegal, breeding higher-yielding corn varieties in Kenya, organizing farm co-ops in Brazil, and helping the Maasai in Tanzania improve their herd management. With the success of the high-yielding grain varieties in India, we were working actively to introduce them in other countries. Managing the IADS was complicated, simply because we were working with the AID, the host-country government, and officials and farmers within the country. On top of this, my earlier responsibility of advising the secretary on foreign agricultural policy continued. For me, this was a stressful and demanding period, but also one of intense learning and, above all else, a chance to improve agriculture on many fronts at once.

I headed the IADS for two years, then in 1968 Richard Nixon was elected president. I knew that I did not want to work in a Nixon administration. I resigned, leaving office a week before Nixon was inaugurated in January 1969. Much to my regret, Nixon dismantled the IADS. The reason given was that U.S. farmers did not want the USDA helping other countries to develop their agriculture, thus creating competition for them.

I had arrived in the department in 1959 and left in early 1969. This was a remarkably intense and rewarding decade. Between 1959 and 1966 my government service grade went from GS-7 to GS-18 and agency head. No one could have asked for more opportunities than I had during this period. Many friendships from then continue to this day. Orville Freeman and I maintained a close relationship until his death at eighty-four in 2003. At the secretary's memorial service, his son, Mike Freeman, made a point of telling me that the secretary had long thought of me as his second son.

I walked away from the Nixon administration, but not from my life's work. The next half century or so would be spent at various institutes, researching and writing about an ever-wider array of global environmental issues.

7

Shifting Gears:
The Overseas Development Council

I had been too busy to think much about what I would do if Hubert Humphrey were to lose the election. And perhaps it was just as well. Shortly after the election in late 1968, I was approached by James P. Grant, a senior official at AID and someone I had worked with a few years earlier when he was the AID mission director in Turkey. Jim had been contacted by a group of U.S. opinion leaders who wanted to start a research organization to focus on third-world development and the U.S. role in it, and asked if he would head it.

After the extraordinary success of the Marshall Plan and the enthusiasm it generated, U.S. public support for international development was waning. The group wanted to create an organization, the Overseas Development Council (ODC), to try to reverse this trend and restore U.S. support for international development efforts. These goals meshed nicely with my sense of what needed to be done.

Jim said he would take this position if I would join him.

Although he had extensive experience with developing countries, he had not had much research experience and was thus looking for help. Jim offered me the position of vice president, but having just been in a management position I indicated a preference for being a senior fellow and concentrating on research. At this point there were many issues that I had been thinking about and wanting to write about. Jim understood. Within a few weeks, we signed a lease for space at 1717 Massachusetts Avenue NW in the heart of Washington's Think Tank Row, and in January 1969 the ODC was born.

This period was a particularly yeasty time in U.S. history. It was in 1969 that the country made good on Kennedy's bold 1961 promise that the United States would land a man on the moon during the decade. The photograph of the earth taken from outer space reminded us that political boundaries, not visible from space, are mere human constructs.

Also serving as part of the political backdrop to everything we did was the divisive, hotly debated Vietnam War. The Cold War between the West, led by the United States, and the Eastern bloc, led by the Soviet Union, was a dominant issue during this era. China, largely in isolation since the communist takeover in 1949, was showing signs of opening up to the outside world.

While I was heading the International Agricultural Development Service, we had our largest overseas technical assistance team in Vietnam—some 200 strong in total. During my first visit there the embassy scheduled a briefing by two Army lieutenants of roughly my age. As the briefing proceeded with maps, charts, troop numbers, body counts, and an overview of U.S. strategy, I remember feeling that it was so superficial—not a winning strategy. Like many others, I began to wonder why we were there.

Within the United States, the 1960s witnessed the emergence of the counterculture, consisting mostly of young, upper-middle-class whites, most of whom were either college graduates or college dropouts, who were challenging the status quo. They were opposed to the war in Vietnam, supported greater gender and racial equality, and wanted freedom to experiment with drugs. Jentri Anders, a social anthropologist, summarized the goals of this movement as "freedom to explore one's potential, freedom to create one's Self, freedom of personal expression, freedom from scheduling, freedom from rigidly defined roles and hierarchical statuses."

On the economic front, the early 1970s saw a dramatic rise in grain prices. This began in the summer of 1972 after the Russians, facing a catastrophic crop failure, cornered the world wheat market by secretly buying up most of the exportable wheat supplies. As this became public knowledge, wheat prices soared and food prices followed. Almost overnight once stable prices became erratic.

Shortly thereafter came the Arab oil export embargo, and oil prices climbed even more. Gasoline became scarce. Television news focused on the long lines of cars at gas stations. From 1950 to 1972, a bushel of wheat could have been traded for a barrel of oil, but between 1972 and 1974 alone, the price of wheat doubled and the price of oil quadrupled. By 1980 it took six bushels of wheat to buy one barrel of oil. From a research vantage point, these were my issues, my cup of tea.

With growing uncertainty about what the future might hold, people were eager for new insights. Analysts were trying to forecast the future, producing a number of books including *Future Shock*, in which Alvin and Heidi Toffler discussed the effects of fast-changing technology. Other influential books looking at the effects of accelerating technological change were Zbigniew Brzezinski's *Between Two Ages* and Ralph Lapp's *The Logarithmic Century*.

The modern environmental movement, spurred by the publication of Rachel Carson's *Silent Spring* in 1962, was gaining momentum. The first Earth Day was held in 1970. More books quickly followed: Charles Reich's *The Greening of America*, Richard Falk's *This Endangered Planet*, and Barry Commoner's *The Closing Circle*. And then in 1972 came *The Limits to Growth* by Donella Meadows, Dennis Meadows, Jørgen Randers, and William W. Behrens III. Other books had begun hinting at potential constraints on economic growth, but while they created waves, *The Limits to Growth* generated a tsunami.

At the launching of *The Limits to Growth* hosted by the Smithsonian Institution and moderated by Elliot Richardson, who was then secretary of health, education, and welfare, I listened with interest as the authors discussed the various limits on economic growth that they had identified and projected. From the beginning, it was clear the business community would attack it. (However, in 2012 when I spoke at the fortieth anniversary of the release of *The Limits to Growth*, I was able to identify in some detail the emerging constraints on the expansion of the food supply, such as shrinking water supplies and the glass ceiling on rice yields in Japan and South Korea and wheat yields in France, Germany, and the United Kingdom. The study's critics had largely disappeared in the intervening years.)

It was against this backdrop that I was shifting from an unbelievably exciting decade in government to one with a whole new range of options. Freed of management responsibilities, I had time to write books and articles and accept speaking invitations on a variety of topics, ranging from the world food prospect to the growing interdependence among countries. New vistas opened for me as I wrote for *The Wall Street Journal*, *Foreign Affairs*, the *Washington Post*, *Science*, and *Scientific American*.

Scientific American, which devoted its annual theme issue in 1970 to the biosphere, invited me to write the article on food. This forced me to organize my thinking about agriculture as a process in the biosphere. What I learned was that not only did *Scientific American* have a huge circulation in its own right, but that it ingeniously marketed individual articles. For starters, the magazine had a four-page marketing pamphlet of some 1,600 articles printed in fine type, each accompanied by a box for checking to order. This list was widely promoted in colleges and universities. Professors could select from these articles to, in effect, assemble their own textbooks, tailor-made for the particular courses they were teaching.

Scientific American also recombined articles from the magazine around various themes, republishing them as *Scientific American* books. For example, my article was included in a collection of food articles and at least four other theme collections including biology, anthropology, civilization, and human nutrition. This was a lesson in marketing that I would later use.

My early months at the ODC were spent writing *Seeds of Change*, a book about the Green Revolution. I had been researching the evolution of the high-yielding dwarf wheats and rices, a process that began in Japan for the wheats and that continued with their adaptation and improvement by Norman Borlaug and his colleagues in Mexico. Japan's dwarf rices were adapted at the International Rice Research Institute (IRRI) under Robert Chandler's leadership for use in other countries. These dwarf short-straw varieties could double yields, partly because much less of the plant's photosynthate was needed to produce the straw, leaving more to produce seed.

While I was working on the food in the biosphere article, Borlaug was awarded the 1970 Nobel Peace Prize for his work on eradicating hunger. *Science* asked me to write the appreciation piece. I began the article like this: "Late in 1944, four young

American scientists assembled in the hills outside Mexico City. Their mission was to export the U.S. agricultural revolution to Mexico. They believed that the application of science to agriculture could achieve the same results in the poor countries as it had in the United States. Like Mao Tse-tung, they believed that the future of these countries would be decided in the countryside."

I concluded the piece by noting that Borlaug's work in developing the new wheats along with high-yielding rices shortly afterward at the IRRI could "affect the well-being of more people in a shorter period of time than any technological advance in history. This is not to imply the new seeds offer a solution to the food problem, but they do buy some precious time, perhaps an additional 10 to 15 years in which to stabilize population growth." Norm, who was a longtime friend, rarely ever gave a talk on the world food prospect in which he did not emphasize the urgency of putting the brakes on population growth.

Two years later, I was invited by the *Saturday Review of Literature*, now defunct, to review *The Limits to Growth*. And though I was not certain about the value of computer modeling to project our future, there was clearly a need for a systemic approach to analyzing global environmental-economic relationships, and it did seem to me that this young team of MIT researchers, led by Dennis and Donella Meadows, were on the right track. Their thinking meshed with my own approach to research, analysis, and policymaking.

In 1973 I did a lengthy piece, "The Need for a World Food Reserve," that appeared on the op-ed page of *The Wall Street Journal*. Not surprisingly, Nixon's secretary of agriculture, Earl Butz, opposed the idea. He argued that the reserve would depress farm prices when in effect it was designed to avoid both price collapses and soaring prices. With a floor price for acquisition and a ceiling price for release, it would offer stability to both consumers and farmers. At this writing, there is again talk about the need for a food reserve. (Since we no longer have cropland idled under U.S. farm programs as we did then, and since climate change is introducing even greater uncertainty in agriculture, the need for that reserve is even more urgent today.)

While my early years at the USDA had been devoted to becoming knowledgeable about world agriculture, shortly after publication of *Man, Land and Food* I began broadening my knowledge about the world in general, and particularly about the relationship between the earth's ecosystem and the world economy. This allowed me to weigh in more effectively when advising governments directly or when outlining policy directions in my research, writing, and speaking.

My next book, *World Without Borders*, was for me a breakout work both in the breadth of issues it covered and the audience it was reaching. It described how the world was tied together by the earth's natural systems, the fast-growing trade and financial links, and their interplay with governments. The bottom line was that the world needed new and stronger international institutions to deal with these linkages. Fortuitously, the international community, led by the United States, created the United Nations Population Fund in 1967 (originally called the United Nations Fund for Population Activities, UNFPA) and, in 1972, the United Nations Environment Programme.

The New Yorker described *World Without Borders* as "an encyclopedic, lucid assessment of some of the world's persistent problems . . . and some carefully documented, highly plausible suggestions for solving them. [Brown] persuasively argues . . . that the day of the militaristic nation state is over, and that a unified global society is the only hope for survival." This book was about globalization well before the concept was widely used.

At this point, with time to broaden my knowledge of the world, I was becoming keenly aware of the expanding role of multinational corporations in the global economy. This was a time not only of world economic growth but of economic integration across national boundaries. Corporations would produce for a world market. Manufacturing supply chains could be anchored in many countries.

To illustrate this point, I constructed an integrated list of countries (measured by gross national product) and corporations (measured by gross annual sales). In the top 50 of this integrated list of 100, countries dominated, with only eight corporations making the top 50. General Motors, the largest corporation, was ranked eighteenth. In the second grouping of 50, there were thirty-six corporations and only fourteen countries. We clearly had entered a new era of increased corporate influence and of globalization.

The title for the book came from a newspaper article in which students in Prague, Czechoslovakia, were interviewed sometime after Soviet tanks had rolled into their city to quell the 1968 uprising. When a student was asked what kind of world she would like, she responded, "A world without borders." The words jumped off the page, capturing the spirit of the book that I was writing.

One manifestation of the growing concern about resource issues and globalization was the organizing of conferences by the United Nations on such topics as population, food, water, and urbanization. Two of these meetings were scheduled in 1974: the World Population Conference, held in Bucharest in August, and the World Food Conference, held in Rome in November. The UNFPA had asked me to write a book for the

Bucharest conference. They wanted a book that dealt with the many dimensions of the population issue, including not only food but other resources and the relationship between social condition and fertility levels. Entitled *In the Human Interest*, this book appeared in English as well as in Arabic, Italian, Indonesian, Japanese, Portuguese, and Spanish.

In late summer, we at the ODC realized that no book had been commissioned for the upcoming food conference. So Erik Eckholm, my research assistant, and I began working fast on a book entitled *By Bread Alone*. As we were coming down the home stretch, we learned that *The New York Times* was planning a series of articles on food for the weeks leading up to the October conference. Erik and I tried to figure out who the various reporters would be, including those who wrote on topics such as agriculture, nutrition, and trade. We sent each of them a copy of the book while it was still in typescript. After several *New York Times* feature articles on food either cited or quoted *By Bread Alone*, editors at the *Times* began restricting such reliance on us.

The USDA, which was also working on a report to be released before the conference, was behind schedule and in the end failed to deliver. The U.N. Food and Agriculture Organization in Rome was producing a background report for the conference as well, but it had little original to say and it largely ignored the population issue. As a result, *By Bread Alone* became the leading source of information for anyone looking for an up-to-date account of the world food situation and future prospects for eradicating hunger.

In 1975, I received a letter from Julius Nyerere, president of Tanzania and one of Africa's elder statesmen. He wrote, "Sometime ago, you sent me a copy of your book, *By Bread Alone*. I had already read your *World Without Borders* and I am writing to congratulate you as well as to thank you, for both books."

He went on to say, "In *By Bread Alone*, you say that 'not two in a hundred of the national political leaders knows that population which increases by 3 percent a year will increase 19 times in a century,' and you may well have been right. But whatever the number who had that knowledge, you have now increased it by at least one! Your example on page 180 struck me very forcibly because the Algerian population of 15 million which you gave as your example is very roughly the same as the present Tanzanian population. That our population may be 288 million in a hundred years makes you (me!) think."

I describe such contacts with historical figures as intersections with history. Another of these came in late 1974 when Eve Labouisse, a member of the Cosmopolitan Club, a prestigious New York women's club, invited me to speak at one of their monthly dinners. Specifically she wanted me to talk about the world food situation, which had become rather chaotic following the crop failure in the Soviet Union.

After accepting the invitation, I learned that my host's full name was Eve Curie Labouisse. She was the daughter of Marie Curie, one of my heroes. Marie Curie was not only the first woman to receive a Nobel Prize, she was also the first of only four scientists to earn two of the coveted awards—the first in physics, shared with her husband, Pierre Curie, and Henri Becquerel in 1903, and the second in chemistry, in 1911.

Although we often think of Marie Curie as French she was actually Polish, née Maria Sklodowska. She came to Paris as a graduate student because Poland did not admit women to graduate schools.

Marie Curie coined the term *radioactivity* and discovered two elements, radium and polonium, the latter named after her homeland. In addition, Eve's sister Irène and her husband, Frédéric Joliot, won the Nobel Prize in Chemistry in 1935 for their synthesis of new radioactive elements. Furthermore, Eve's husband, Henry Labouisse, accepted the Nobel Peace Prize in 1965 on behalf of UNICEF, which he headed from 1965 to 1979.

Eve was fond of apologizing because she was the only member of the family who did not have a Nobel Prize. Born in Paris on December 6, 1904, she had become a concert pianist and then, during World War II, played an active role in the French resistance. A woman of many talents, she wrote a widely acclaimed biography of her mother that was published in 1937, not long after her mother's death, a book I had read as a teenager.

At about this time, I was on a flight from London to Dulles Airport (outside Washington, DC) in, as I recall, one of the early Boeing 747 jumbo transports. My seat was next to the window. On my immediate right was an elderly woman. She had with her some packages wrapped in brown paper that she was trying to put under her seat. I indicated that they should be pushed under the seat in front of her, which I helped her do. After she was seated, she was trying to find the light switch, so I explained how to operate the light. It seemed clear to me that she was not a very experienced traveler. As we talked on the flight, she referred to her son David and what he was doing. I then realized that she was Alice Acheson, widow of President Harry Truman's secretary of state, Dean Acheson.

She was returning from Iran, where she had been touring archeological sites with two guides, both leading U.K. academics on ancient Persian culture. The items she had wrapped in brown paper were small, rare Persian rugs given to her by the shah of Iran during her visit.

A week or so later, I got a phone call from Mrs. Acheson asking if I was indeed the young man who had helped her get her Persian carpets through customs. I indicated that I was. She then asked if I could attend a dinner two weeks hence. I replied that I would be delighted to do so. Some days later she called and said that it would be a black tie affair. Not long before the dinner, she called again to say she had arranged for me to have a dinner partner. She turned out to be Janet Murrow, the widow of Edward R. Murrow, a pioneer among television talk show hosts, and since Joseph Alsop, a leading newspaper columnist, was there, we ended up discussing the world food situation, which was a live issue at the time.

During the ODC years, I addressed many conferences, some of them in what for me were exotic places, such as Aspen, Colorado, and Salzburg, Austria. In Aspen, the conferences usually focused on energy and food. During the early 1970s the Aspen Institute organized the Great Ideas seminars for corporate executives. These were two-week periods of intense exposure to great ideas, a concept inspired by Mortimer Adler, a professor of philosophy at the University of Chicago. One of these Great Ideas seminars, held in the summer of 1972, was chaired by Bill Moyers, who asked me to be his assistant. It was here that I met Roger and Vicki Sant, who years later provided the start-up grant to launch the Earth Policy Institute in 2001.

In 1971 and again in 1974 I was invited to be on the faculty of the Salzburg Seminar in American Studies. This series was designed to expose promising young midcareer Europeans, mostly in government but including some in industry as well, to American culture and thinking. The seminar was held in Schloss Leopoldskron, the elegant home where *The Sound of Music* was filmed. In 1971, Shirley and I attended. In 1974, Brian and Brenda, who were thirteen and eight, accompanied me.

At one of the dinner discussions among Salzburg faculty members, I suggested that we challenge the students to a race around the lake, roughly two miles. The group quickly agreed. Princeton economist John Lewis, who was chairman of the faculty and someone I knew from his years in New Delhi, announced that the faculty were challenging the students, most of whom were in their late twenties or early thirties, to a race around the lake. The "faculty," of course, was me. John had no intention of running, nor did any other faculty member. In any event, the date was scheduled. This event became a social focus of our three-week seminar as people speculated about the prospects for various fellows, some of whom were experienced distance runners.

One of the more promising entrants was a very athletic, well-conditioned Romanian who was a member of his country's white-water kayak team. Another was a young German who had been an 800-meter runner in college. There was also a lean, young Canadian in attendance who looked like he could be a formidable competitor. As the race started, the pace was unusually fast, one I knew I could not sustain. Either the field was going to leave me behind or they were overcommitting in the early stages of the run, perhaps because no one knew quite what to expect from the other runners. I adjusted my pace based on the latter assumption, knowing that I needed to slow down to retain any chance of winning. As we approached the far side of the lake, which people could see from the Schloss grounds, I was in fourth place. Then slowly, one by one, I picked off the Romanian, the German, and, finally, with a few hundred yards to go, the Canadian.

When running on the far side of the lake, I could hear Brenda yelling, "Go, Daddy, go!" It was a fun occasion, one that I particularly enjoyed sharing with Brian and Brenda.

Meanwhile, the two books and the articles I had written were generating many speaking opportunities. During the last few months in 1974, for example, I gave talks at a Nobel conference in Stockholm, a meeting of the Club of Rome in Berlin, the World Food Conference in Rome, and an international nutrition conference in Guatemala. The flow of speaking invitations has continued ever since.

Among the more interesting experiences during my time at the ODC was my inclusion in the notorious Nixon White House "enemies list." Even today I'm not certain why my name was on the list, but I do know that associated with that listing was a break-in at my townhouse in Chevy Chase, Maryland, one in which drawers were pulled out and turned upside down, everything dumped onto the floor. As best as I could tell, however, nothing was missing. My office was also broken into. Being on the list promised one more thing: a complimentary audit of your income taxes by the Internal Revenue Service. My sense was that these were measures designed to intimidate those who in some way actively opposed the president's policies.

The sad part of this period was that my marriage was coming to an end. We separated for a year as Shirley returned to Wyoming with the children. We had actually talked about the advantages of their growing up in ranch country as opposed to the Maryland suburbs of Washington, DC, but never in terms of actually separating. A year later, we divorced amicably, maintaining a joint checking account for years to come.

My six years at the ODC were intellectually rich ones. I was given great freedom by Jim Grant in selecting research topics and the books that I would write. Jim left it to me to set my own research and writing priorities, continuing in the tradition of Quentin West, John Schnittker, and Orville Freeman by creating a working environment where the only constraints on what I could contribute were those imposed by my personal limitations.

Working with Jim broadened my horizon because of his experience and vision of the world. To begin with, he was born in Peking (Beijing), where his father was for fifteen years a professor of public health at the Rockefeller Foundation–funded Peking Union Medical College. Jim's work in the late 1940s with the United Nations Relief and Rehabilitation Administration in China, his stint as the U.S. AID mission director in Turkey from 1964 until 1967, and his time in Washington as assistant administrator of the U.S. AID for Vietnam from 1967 to 1969 helped prepare him to lead the ODC. He was a visionary. Jim made the ODC a focal point for development research, seminars, and conferences—in short, a place for the international development community.

But his crowning glory was to come after he left the ODC in 1980 to head UNICEF. In this capacity, he took the vaccination of children and the use of oral rehydration therapy to treat childhood diarrhea to a whole new level. It was an extraordinary achievement by a U.N. agency and a tribute to Jim's ability to persuade national political leaders to take the health and development of children seriously. *New York Times* columnist Nicholas D. Kristof wrote in 2008 that Jim "probably saved more lives than were destroyed by Hitler, Mao, and Stalin combined" through this work.

As my thinking and writing ranged widely during these years with Jim, it became clear to me that negative environmental trends were emerging as a major threat to our future and that protecting our environment would become the great issue of our time. It was also clear that this issue deserved a research institute of its own. Another chapter was about to begin.

8

The Worldwatch Institute:
Present at the Creation

Late one summer afternoon in 1973 in Aspen, Colorado, after the day's meetings were over and the sun was slanting behind the mountains, Bill Dietel of the Rockefeller Brothers Fund (RBF) and I were the only ones left in the swimming pool. As we chatted, we discovered that we both sensed the need for a research institute to work on global environmental issues.

Bill suggested that I write up a description of what such an organization would look like and send it to him to critique. It should be short—much like an informal grant proposal. Not long after, I sent him a six-page, double-spaced description of the proposed research institute and how it would function.

Bill responded with a few minor suggestions, and I then formally submitted a request for a $500,000 start-up grant. Some months went by without a decision, largely because the brothers who controlled the funding were somewhat divided. John D. Rockefeller III, whose big issue was population, was supportive.

So apparently was Laurance, who was concerned with conservation issues. But David, the banker, and Nelson, the politician and the dominant member of the group, were not convinced. Then came what I would later see as a fortuitous break.

In December 1973, Nelson had resigned as governor of New York, presumably to prepare to run for the Republican presidential nomination in 1976. To aid in this effort, he set up the Commission on Critical Choices for Americans—a vehicle that would enable him to analyze a broad set of policy issues ranging from education to foreign policy. Among the more than forty distinguished members of the panel were Edward Teller, Norman Borlaug, George Shultz, Bess Myerson, and Sol Linowitz.

As the months went by, however, his commission came under public criticism. Although it was indeed discussing critical choices for the country, the discussions were always in private—no public participation, no progress reports, no transparency. Nelson realized that he needed to have a meeting that would be open to at least a select public, including trusted members of the press. It was to be a two-day conference, held at the LBJ Library in Austin, Texas, in April 1974. The meeting would be hosted by Lady Bird Johnson, who was indebted to Laurance Rockefeller for his active support of her national beautification project. Because high grain prices and overall instability in the world food economy were an issue at the time, they invited me to talk about the world agricultural prospect.

Lady Bird introduced Nelson, who welcomed the group and introduced me. Responding to both the historic nature and setting of this event, with Nelson Rockefeller in effect going public with what was widely seen as his bid for the Republican presidential nomination, and with LBJ looking down on us from the murals on the library's twenty-foot walls, I was firing on all four cylinders. The talk, which explained the dramatic rise in world grain prices and discussed the measures needed to stabilize them, elicited a strong positive response from the group.

After I spoke, a number of other speakers, much more academic in style, failed to stir the audience. As a result, the press coverage focused on my talk, including an Associated Press story and a column by James Reston in *The New York Times*. Both were widely picked up across the country. Some months later, Reston's column was expanded into an article in *Reader's Digest*.

Nelson, who was thoroughly pleased with my address, now felt indebted to me. When the RBF board met in June 1974, they quickly approved the half-million-dollar start-up grant. I then moved ahead with my remaining obligations to the Overseas Development Council (ODC), which included talks at the World Population Conference in Bucharest in August and the World Food Conference in Rome in November. My goal was to wrap everything up by late November.

At the heart of the staff for this new organization, which we called the Worldwatch Institute, were Erik Eckholm, my ODC research assistant, and Blondeen Duhaney (later Gravely), my administrative assistant. Blondeen was a vital force. In 1965, shortly after graduating from high school in North Carolina as valedictorian, she moved to Washington, DC, and began working with me in the secretary's office at the U.S. Department of Agriculture. We bonded immediately. Her vivacity and energetic work style endeared her to all who worked with her. Worldwatch took our working relationship to another level as she became the institute's office manager—taking the lead in setting up the new organization—and later vice president for administration. We worked together in various capacities for twenty-nine years until she had to take medical retirement due to suffering with lupus, an autoimmune disease.

Newly recruited researchers included James Fallows, former editor of the *Harvard Crimson*; Kathleen Newland, a recent graduate of the Princeton master's program in public affairs; and Denis Hayes, the coordinator of Earth Day in 1970. I convinced Bruce Stokes, whom I had met at the 1974 World Food Conference in Rome, to abandon his master's program at the Columbia School of Journalism to head up our office of information.

Kathleen Courrier, a freelancer, was our part-time editor in the early years. When she took a full-time job, Linda Starke, who was on our outreach staff, became our editor. She went on to edit all our books and monographs. Shortly after she left in 1982 to begin her own freelance editing business, I enlisted her for the annual *State of the World* reports that we launched in 1984. (More on these later.) With those reports under her belt, she was very much in demand to edit various international commission reports, in effect becoming a jet-set editor.

Felix Gorrell, who was comptroller of the Brookings Institution, advised us during the early years and also served as our treasurer. His assistance with investing and accounting was invaluable. Orville Freeman agreed to serve as chairman of the board. In late November 1974 we moved into our new quarters on the seventh floor of 1776 Massachusetts Avenue NW, just across the street from Brookings and the ODC.

These early years were exciting. We were fashioning a new genre of research institute, one that did interdisciplinary research. This would not be a traditional economic or international affairs research institution, but rather one whose research centered on the environment broadly defined but that also included food, energy, population, water, and particularly the relationship between the environment and the economy. Our goal was to make our published material accessible to lay readers, publishable in scientific magazines, useful to the media, and indispensable to policymakers. We were caught up in the excitement of this challenge.

We also envisioned Worldwatch serving a worldwide constituency, a goal that only added to the complexity of the challenge. It is one thing to study global issues; it is another to reach a global population with the research results.

We decided early on that we would have two research products: a monograph series, which we called the Worldwatch Papers, typically thirty to seventy pages, and books. The Worldwatch Paper series enabled us to produce studies on key issues in a relatively short period of time. Remembering what I had learned from *Scientific American* about making multiple use of research products, much of what was in the papers eventually would be incorporated into books, which could be translated and published in other languages.

Not only do book publishers provide a means of reaching people in other languages, but they pay for the rights to do so. The other side of this coin, of course, is that you have to produce books that are of sufficient relevance to justify their publication in other languages.

I decided that our first publication should be written by someone other than me largely because I did not want Worldwatch to be seen as the Lester Brown Institute. Erik, who had assisted me with *In the Human Interest* and coauthored *By Bread Alone* at the ODC, was ready to roll. He moved fast and finished *Losing Ground: Environmental Stress and World Food Prospects* in the fall of 1975, in time for publication in early 1976. *Losing Ground* broadened the near-exclusive focus in the environmental community on industrial pollution in the developed world to include deforestation, overgrazing, soil erosion, desertification, and other environmental threats in the developing world.

While the book was at our publisher, Erik pulled material from it on the fast-growing demand for firewood, expanding it into the first in the monograph series. Entitled *The Other Energy Crisis: Firewood*, Worldwatch Paper 1 was published in September 1975. It was a huge media hit, generating a ton of stories, including a front-page story in *The New York Times*. The key to its success was the juxtaposition of the firewood crisis—affecting a third of humanity, but largely below the radar—with the oil crisis—of which the industrial countries were, at a time of quadrupling oil prices, keenly aware.

The analysis in this first paper sent ripples through the world forestry community. It resulted in a restructuring of the World Bank's forestry lending. It also led the government of Indonesia to add a firewood component to its national forestry program. The institute was off and running.

When *Losing Ground* was released in early 1976, George Brockway, the head of W. W. Norton & Company, called it an instant classic. In addition to extensive media coverage from the press launch and translation into the world's leading languages, almost every chapter in *Losing Ground* was reprinted in one or another widely read periodical—everything from *Science* magazine to the Sunday Outlook section of the *Washington Post*. We had quickly reached one of our goals: a depth of analysis and style of writing that was publishable in both scientific journals and the popular press.

Not long after publication of *Losing Ground*, when Erik was on a field trip in Nepal gathering information on the deterioration of mountain environments, he spent a couple of days in a rural district outside Kathmandu. The district leader was so impressed with *Losing Ground* that he decided to make a copy, but not with a copying machine, because they did not exist—at least not in the villages of Nepal. He used a typewriter with a team of typists typing around the clock for the entire two days and two nights that Erik was in the village.

Erik had set the bar high for the institute. All of our papers did well, but our next megahit was Worldwatch Paper 5, *Twenty-Two Dimensions of the Population Problem*, by Bruce Stokes, Patricia McGrath, and me. We went beyond the exclusive focus on population and food bequeathed to us by Thomas Malthus to focus on the many effects of population growth including housing, water, health services, forests, and access to national recreation areas. Malthus believed that population would increase geometrically while the food supply would increase arithmetically.

The monograph devoted three pages or so to each dimension of the population problem, and, where data were available, a graph showing the appropriate trend and how it was being altered by population growth. Many international development organizations distributed the paper by the thousands to their employees. And, unheard of for a monograph, it was translated into several leading languages, including Arabic, French, Spanish, Japanese, Indonesian, Portuguese, and Italian. It also appeared in less widely spoken languages, such as Burmese and Nepalese. The Nepalis printed 10,000 copies of their edition.

The extraordinary success of this monograph, which eventually hit 186,000 copies in print in all languages, was the result of looking at the population issue through a fresh lens, an interdisciplinary lens. This was also a time when the world was beginning to focus on the relationship between population growth and environmental issues, particularly the loss of biological diversity.

Meanwhile, Denis Hayes produced several Worldwatch Papers in rapid succession, including *Energy: The Case for Con-*

servation and *Nuclear Power: The Fifth Horseman.* In the latter he made a convincing argument based on economics alone that nuclear power was not a viable option. These and some Worldwatch Papers on solar energy were incorporated into the book *Rays of Hope,* another pioneering work.

Kathleen Newland produced two Worldwatch Papers: *Women in Politics: A Global Review* and *Women and Population Growth: Choice Beyond Childbearing.* These provided the foundation for her book, *The Sisterhood of Man,* which emphasized the importance of providing girls and women with equal opportunities and linked these opportunities and rising female education with falling fertility.

During these early years I produced several Worldwatch Papers. One of them, which I was particularly pleased with, *Redefining National Security,* was published in October 1977. Robert Redford, an environmentalist from early on, who dropped by our office from time to time, called me from Dulles Airport one day to say that he had just finished reading it and thought it was a landmark work. More than a decade was to pass before *Foreign Affairs* published its first article on redefining security.

So many of the papers were wildly successful that I can mention only a few. An analysis coauthored by Ted Wolf and me on the need to reverse the environmental deterioration that was increasing hunger and malnutrition in Africa (*Reversing Africa's Decline*) was widely used by the World Bank, which distributed 900 copies to its senior management staff in Washington and all its professionals working on Africa. The bank also organized seminars on the paper for its staff and translated it into French for mass distribution in Africa's Francophone countries. The African Development Bank invited Ted and me to conduct a two-day seminar for its senior staff and executive directors at its headquarters in Abidjan in the Ivory Coast.

In January 1989, when British Prime Minister Margaret Thatcher decided to host an international conference of political leaders on the future of the ozone layer, her staff discovered that they did not have a document outlining the origins of the problem, the trends, the responses called for, or the economic effects of various responses. So they ordered 200 copies of Worldwatch Paper 87, *Protecting Life on Earth: Steps to Save the Ozone Layer,* by Cynthia Pollock Shea. If a government of an advanced industrial society, such as the United Kingdom, lacked the research organization to deal with such basic issues, we could only wonder about governments elsewhere.

Early on we developed an extensive mailing list of opinion leaders to get complimentary copies of the papers. We had what we called "paper stuffings," where everyone on the staff sat on the floor and stuffed the addressed envelopes. We turned the task into a social occasion, often heckling the author. We also opened the bar every Friday afternoon at 5 p.m. for an institute happy hour.

In these early Worldwatch years I also wrote *The Twenty-Ninth Day.* Published in early 1978, it is for me one of the favorites among my books. The book's title comes from a riddle that the French use to teach schoolchildren exponential growth. If a lily pond has one lily leaf in it the first day, two the second, and four the third, and if the number of leaves continues to double each day and the pond fills on the thirtieth day, when is it half full? Answer: the twenty-ninth day. The book title was intended to convey the urgency with which we need to deal with our growing claims on this finite planet. It was one of the first books to discuss in detail our dependence on the earth's natural systems and carrying capacity.

In the spring following the book's release, I was scheduled to do an interview on NBC's *Today* show with Jane Pauley. The interview, which ran between 7:45 and 8:00 a.m., was referred to several times with a teaser during the preceding hour. It said, "Today we have an author who has written a book on soil erosion. That's right! Soil erosion." For days afterward Brian and Brenda went around the house saying, "And our dad has written a book on soil erosion. That's right! Soil erosion."

In sales, translations, and media citations—by every criterion we used—*The Twenty-Ninth Day* was a smashing success. A glowing review by David Burns on the front page of the *Washington Post* book review assured that it got off to a fast start. Appearing in some twenty languages, it focused global attention on our dependence on four natural systems—forests, grasslands, fisheries, and croplands—and their carrying capacity. It was a pioneering work on the concept of sustainable development.

In 1981, I expanded my ideas in *Building a Sustainable Society*. It, too, was widely translated and used in the environmental and development fields. Even the Soviets were paying dollars for language rights to our books.

One of the criteria by which we evaluated our performance was whether we were producing research products of interest to the media. We knew we were getting extraordinary media coverage, but I wanted to get a more precise sense of our effectiveness. To do this, I checked how often we had been cited in *The New York Times* each year, compared with other prominent research organizations. These included Resources for the Future, the Brookings Institution, and two leading conservative think tanks, the American Enterprise Institute and the Hudson Institute. In 1976, our first full year of publishing, we quickly jumped ahead of all the research institutes except the venerated grandfather of public policy research institutes, Brookings. It took us four more years to overtake Brookings in

New York Times citations. Since the Brookings' staff was at least ten times the size of Worldwatch's, surpassing them was not a trivial matter.

This, of course, was only *The New York Times* and the United States. We were also interested in how much our research was covered by major news organizations in other countries and in the global outlets, such as the BBC, Voice of America, and later CNN, along with the principal newswires, especially the Associated Press and Reuters. Our clipping service indicated we were either publishing or being cited in several stories a day worldwide. We were being taken seriously.

Another test was whether we were reaching a global constituency. The answer to this question was evident in the many translations of our books. What we did not anticipate was that so many Worldwatch Papers would be translated into other languages and that some of them would have print runs in excess of 100,000 copies. Our interdisciplinary or systemic approach to analyzing global environmental issues, broadly defined, was enthusiastically received. We were actually doing what we had set out to do.

As Worldwatch neared the end of its sixth year, RBF did a review of how effectively their investment had been used. Their conclusion: "In sum, Worldwatch is making a significant contribution to the way policymakers in this and other countries look at their resources and make decisions that affect their use.... Few other models—Rand, Brookings, ... or the American Enterprise Institute—have matched the force of the ideas and research Worldwatch is now communicating to those responsible for our fate."

Reaching a global constituency is, the report noted, "an infinitely more complex undertaking than merely reaching a national constituency." The author of the RBF report talked to many journalists. The report said, "Among news reporters, it is hard to find anyone who is anything but enthusiastic about Worldwatch and its services." Among the many it cited were Walter Sullivan and Bayard Webster, science writers at *The New York Times*, and Stan Benjamin, a Washington-based science reporter for the Associated Press.

There was the occasional critic. Dennis Flanagan, managing editor at *Scientific American*, said Worldwatch material "is welcome here; it is well researched, and the reports are worthwhile. . . . [But] Les Brown takes a doomsday approach to the environment that we don't buy."

The RBF report also reviewed the management practices that I used at Worldwatch, which were unconventional. For example, we had few staff meetings and we did not have an operating budget. I merely estimated expenditures for the year ahead. Our fiscal policy was a simple one: we would not write any checks that could not be covered. In bypassing the detailed budgeting process, we did not need a budget officer. Perhaps more important, when we decided to do a book or a Worldwatch Paper, I didn't have to ask the individual staff researchers to spend time doing a detailed project budget and finding sources of funding.

Writing about Worldwatch in 1977, the science adviser to the Science Council of Canada said, "There isn't one ounce of fat in that organization. . . . I'm a bit jealous when I see how much [Brown] has produced in such a short time with such a small infrastructure."

The bottom line of this approach is that during the twenty-six years I headed Worldwatch, we never had any staff cutbacks as a result of fiscal stresses or for any other reasons. It may have been unorthodox, but it created an extraordinarily lean, efficient organization. Another unconventional policy for a research institute was my goal of covering part of our budget from income earned from publication sales, book royalties, and speaking fees. We applied the market test to our research products. RBF watched these trends with a certain fascination.

In 1982 RBF set up a committee to oversee and formalize the shift of the fund's management from the brothers' to the cousins' generation. The brothers were getting older, and the Rockefellers in the cousins' generation, including Larry, David Jr., and Neva R. Goodwin, were experienced enough in the family's philanthropy to take charge. I was invited to one of the meetings to talk about issues. They asked the usual questions: How do we get the biggest bang for the buck? How can we make a difference with the limited resources that we have?

At the end of this meeting, Larry Rockefeller, son of Laurance, indicated that the next time I came to New York he would like to get together for a drink and to brainstorm. In the discussion we had some weeks later, I suggested, among other things, that they commission someone to do a report card, sort of an annual physical of the earth, checking its vital signs. I promptly forgot about this. But some months later, Bill Dietel, by then the president of RBF, came to see me. He said they liked the idea of doing an annual report card for the planet, and he wondered if we would be interested in doing it. I demurred. Although the idea had originated with me, I did not particularly want to do it. While at the ODC, I saw how the annual *Agenda for Development* absorbed staff time, often allowing individuals to avoid other potentially more demanding and productive undertakings.

Before long Bill came back and asked if I would reconsider. Bill's persistence paid off. This time I agreed, but with the understanding that he would help us find some additional financial resources. A new era was about to begin.

We had at that time a team of only five researchers, including me, and a total staff of eleven. Adding this annual volume to our existing workload would require more staff and more money. Bill agreed to help with the fundraising. For the initial report, I wrote seven chapters and the other researchers did the remaining four.

In April 1984, we released the first *State of the World* report. It was a stunning success. Our sole reference point in judging its performance was the World Bank's annual *World Development Report (WDR)*. Thus, our goal was to one day publish *State of the World* in as many languages and sell as many copies as the *WDR*. Much to our surprise, the very first edition of *State of the World* surpassed it coming out of the blocks in both translations and sales, and by a wide margin.

State of the World 1984 got off to a quick start, appearing in Chinese, Japanese, and Spanish, among the major languages, and Malaysian, Polish, and Thai among the less widely spoken languages. The U.S. Information Agency, an organization that promoted relevant U.S. publications abroad, sponsored an English edition in India. For the 1985 edition, we added Indonesian. Within four years, *State of the World* was appearing in virtually every major language.

Many magazines and newspapers published excerpts from these reports because they contained so much fresh information and established the links between global environmental, economic, and social trends. Some fifty excerpts were published from the English edition alone of the first *State of the World*. This, combined with reviews and news coverage of the other language editions, added up to a massive release of environmental information worldwide.

Although not designed for classroom use, *State of the World* was unbelievably popular on college campuses. Course adoptions climbed higher each year. By 1991, a total of 1,379 professors were using *State of the World* in their courses at 633 U.S. colleges and universities. In Canada, some fifty universities were using it. So were universities in several other countries. In

Finland, *State of the World* was required reading in each of its eleven universities.

Within the United States, the University of Michigan emerged as our leading adopter when professors used *State of the World 1991* in seventeen courses. Close behind in usage were Michigan State University, the University of Colorado, Cornell University, and the University of California.

State of the World was also used as a "book in common" for incoming college freshmen. Slippery Rock State University in Pennsylvania used the book during its orientation for its 2,300 incoming students in the fall of 1991. Broome Community College in New York State used it in an introductory program for all 2,000 freshmen. Clearly *State of the World* had found a home in the world of higher education.

What was astounding was the variety of courses adopting *State of the World* either as a primary or supplemental text. We compiled a list of forty-five colleges where it had been adopted, but each for a course in a different field of study. Just to cite a few, at Montana State University, the course was Technology and Society. At the University of Tennessee, it was Natural Resource Management. At the University of Maine, it was Contemporary World Issues. At the University of North Carolina, World Population Problems. And at the University of Arizona, Environmental Biology.

We could never get data on course adoptions in China, though from *State of the World 1984* onward nearly all of our books were published there. However, several years ago when I was preparing to give an evening lecture at the China Agricultural University in Beijing, a school with 17,000 students, the president of the university and I had a leisurely prelecture dinner. As we walked from his office to the lecture hall, he told me that every student on campus knew my name because they had read my book *Who Will Feed China?* (see Chapter 10) I was a bit skeptical. He proceeded to validate his point. To our right as we walked to the lecture hall were a couple of card tables where the student drama group was selling tickets for an upcoming event. He went up to them and introduced me, and each of the students immediately recognized my name.

State of the World 1984 caught the attention of Ted Turner. In the spring of 1984, four years after he launched CNN, the first cable news network, I got a phone call from Ted. He was coming to Washington the following week and wondered if we could meet. He said *State of the World* was the most important book he'd read in years. During our meeting, it quickly became clear that Ted was as concerned about global environmental issues and their long-term consequences as I was. We were instant soul mates.

From Washington, Ted was flying to New York to address a meeting of foreign correspondents. He left carrying two cartons of *State of the World*—one under each arm—that he planned to distribute to the correspondents. This was my first contact with Ted, but it would not be the last. He has promoted and distributed my books ever since. In fact, after this meeting, he began an annual distribution of *State of the World* to CNN's worldwide network of reporters. More important, this meeting was the beginning of a lasting friendship.

The *State of the World* report was the right publication at the right time. It was launched when there was a worldwide hunger not only for environmental information but for integrated research that linked environmental trends to other issues like population, natural resources, technology, and international relations. Further, in the absence of an annual U.N. world environmental report, *State of the World* achieved semiofficial status. It was used by governments throughout the world as a basic reference. Thank you, Bill Dietel, for your persistence. Thank you for valuing my idea more than I did.

In 1985, shortly after the second *State of the World* came out, we were contacted by Linda Harrar of the PBS *NOVA* series, based at WGBH in Boston. She wanted to produce a ten-hour television series based on *State of the World*. This represented a unique marriage between a research institute and a public television group. The fundraising, production, and editing of the series and its scheduling for public television took several years. The resulting *Race to Save the Planet* first aired in the fall of 1990, narrated by Meryl Streep.

On a personal note, during this time my son Brian came to work with us. He had become a member of the U.S. Slalom Kayak Team. Since the team training site was on the Potomac River near Washington, he moved to the area and I hired him part-time at the institute to do administrative chores.

During this period we regularly shared lunches, discussing paddling technique, training regimes, the psychology of competition, and other things of mutual interest. Like so many men who as boys aspired to athletic greatness, I was vicariously sharing the experience with him.

Although nearly all my energy was devoted to Worldwatch, I did become involved, in off-hours, in the most intense political campaign of my life: gaining admission for women to the Cosmos Club as full members. When I was admitted in 1969, I was the youngest member of the club, part of a generation that had a strong commitment to gender equity.

The Cosmos Club in Washington, DC, was incorporated in 1878 and patterned after the English men's social clubs, but membership was based not on social standing but on merit, on "scholarship, creative genius or intellectual distinction." The club has counted among its members fifty-six Pulitzer Prize winners and thirty-two Nobel Prize winners. If it were strictly a social club, then restricting membership to men, women, or any other defined group would be fine, but if merit was the basis for membership, then it seemed to me that we could not exclude women.

The club management, which was self-perpetuating, was overwhelmingly opposed to admitting women. But some members thought this position was no longer appropriate. In 1980, I helped organize the "committee of concerned members." I coordinated a survey of individual members, asking their position on this issue. The responses, which were sent to my office at Worldwatch, gave us valuable information for use in the campaign. It was a tough fight. Even getting the club mailing list was difficult. Some members supporting the admission of women broke the rules and took the issue to the press, which intensified pressure on the management.

As stresses intensified between the pro- and anti-women factions, some members resigned. One member was threatened with expulsion. I received a warning letter from the club leadership. Finally in June 1988 as pressures continued to mount, the dam broke and the club voted almost unanimously to admit women. To me it felt like Neil Armstrong's giant leap for mankind.

As the *State of the World* reports began taking off, in 1986 I hired Reah Janise Battenfield (now Kauffman) as my administrative assistant. She came from Michigan State University, where she had been an editor and technical writer—skills that would serve me well. I had no idea at the time just how invaluable she would become as an associate and friend. Among Reah Janise's other talents, she is an excellent seamstress. She makes the warm corduroy jackets that I wear in winter. She also delights in converting colorful fabrics into clip-on bow ties, the only ties that I wear.

In the wake of the extraordinary success of *State of the World*, I began to see a need for another publication, a magazine, preferably one published every two months. This would provide an outlet for short pieces on topical issues. From time to time, we would come up with an idea we wanted to get out more quickly than researching and writing a Worldwatch Paper would permit. A magazine would also enable us to cover in more detail specific facets of larger issues we were working on in a way that could be of interest.

In discussing the bimonthly, which we ended up calling simply *World Watch*, I talked with Susie Buffett, wife of Warren Buffett, about providing support for the magazine. Susie was definitely interested and excited about the prospect, particularly as it came on the heels of our highly successful launch of *State of the World*. Warren, however, was not nearly as enthusiastic. He was at that time serving on the board of the Washington Post Company, which also published *Newsweek* magazine. He had seen too many problems in the magazine field to share our excitement about launching a new one.

Despite the lack of support from Warren, we moved ahead. The initial issue was slated for January/February 1988. Jim Gorman, the first editor of the magazine, served for four years. He was followed by Ed Ayres, the founding editor of *Running Times*. Despite the challenge for all of us, our expectations were exceeded. Within a few years, *World Watch* was appearing in Japanese, Chinese, and Italian. German, French, and Spanish were in the works. We had not anticipated the extent of the international interest and had not even contemplated the prospect of the magazine's appearing in other languages. Once again we were breaking new ground.

Doing the magazine enabled us to hold press events on the lead story each time a new issue was released. These, too, proved to be remarkably successful. Some of the individual magazine articles had a global impact. One of the most attention-getting was "Who Will Feed China?" published in the September/October 1994 issue. (See Chapter 10.)

The Brown Family:
Carl, Mom, Lester, Pop, Marion.

Carl and Lester, 1940.

The Brown family farm, current day.

Stow Creek elementary school graduates. Lester is second from the left back row, 1947. Teacher Henrietta Tomlinson in center rear.

The Brown family: Brian, Brenda, Shirley, and Lester.

Marion razzing Lester at his 60th birthday party at the Cosmos Club. Carl waits his turn. March 1994. *Photo by Rita Malone.*

Lester with his extended Brown family, 2009, taken at reception following the Smithsonian Museum of American History event, *A Conversation with Lester Brown*. L to r: Darlene Rosenberger, niece; brother-in-law Bob Spence, sister Marion Spence; Brian; Alison Dance; granddaughter Bridget; grandniece Olivia Rosenberger; Maureen Kuwano Hinkle; granddaughter Lena; sister-in-law Mary Lou Brown; brother Carl; Brenda; and grandson Cash (front). *Photo by Hugh Talman.*

Farmer Brown loading a tractor trailer
with 600 baskets of tomatoes, 1958.

The "Towers" living group on the
College of Agriculture campus,
Rutgers University, 1953.

On the Queen Frederica,
a Greek ship, ready to sail from
New York to Bombay, 1956.

Lester and Mongol, a local
wrestling champion, prepare
to wrestle. India 1956.

Lester's "sisters" teaching him numbers in Marathi.

Secretary of Agriculture Orville Freeman and Lester in early 1966 at the White House for a Sunday night meeting on the food crisis in India.

Lester being congratulated by President Lyndon Johnson in the Oval Office on receiving the Ten Outstanding Young Men in Federal Service award, 1965.

World Without Borders (1972), a pioneering work on globalization, published when Lester was at the Overseas Development Council.

A *Meet the Press* one-hour special on the world food situation in 1974 with host Laurence Spivak (standing), Earl Butz, Secretary of Agriculture, John Hannah, Administrator of AID (front row). Jean Mayer of Tufts University, Sterling Wortman of the Rockefeller Foundation, and Lester (back row).
Photo by Reni Newsphotos, Inc.

Lester speaking at Planete Terre conference sponsored by
French President Francois Mitterand, June 12, 1989, Paris.

Worldwatch Press Symposium, Earth Summit, Rio de Janeiro, June 1992.
Sandra Postel (front), Ketil Gravir (World Watch Norden) at the podium,
Gro Harlem Brundtland (Prime Minister of Norway), and Lester. *Photo by
Mark Edwards/Still Pictures.*

Inaugural ceremony of a permanent exhibit of Lester's books at Martin Hall, Cook College of Agriculture, Rutgers University, 2005. Beside Lester is Keith Cooper, Executive Dean of Research and Graduate Programs. *Photo by Maureen Kuwano Hinkle.*

Blondeen Gravely and Lester at Earth Policy Institute office before Lester's 70th birthday dinner celebration with friends and family, 2004.

Commencement speaker at Westminster College, Pennsylvania, 2001, where Lester received an honorary degree, one of twenty-five he now holds.

Receiving Sasakawa Environment Award, Stockholm, June 5, 1989. Mostalfa Tolba, Director-General UN Environment Programme; Lester; Pastrano Borrero, former president of Columbia and Chairman of Sasakawa Environment Award Committee.

Receiving the Worldwide Fund for Nature Gold Medal from Prince Philip, 1989.

The Worldwatch Institute team, 1994.

Lester in 1988 with early editions of *State of the World*.
Photo by Steve Gottlieb.

Speaking at the European Parliament, Brussels, 1991.

Lester with longtime friend, Ion Iliescu, President of Romania, 1996.

Lester being interviewed by Turkish television at the World Economic Forum in Davos, Switzerland, 2006.
Photo by Maureen Kuwano Hinkle.

Lester presents the Hindi edition of *Plan B 3.0* to Prime Minister Manmohan Singh of India in 2008.
Photo by Ranjit Barthakur and Samir Menon.

The books have arrived! Unloading cartons of *Plan B 3.0* (Lester, Jonathan Dorn, and Janet Larsen).

EPI Staff 2012. Back row, l to r: Millicent Johnson, Emily Adams, Matt Roney, Lester Brown. Front row: Reah Janise Kauffman, Julianne Simpson, Janet Larsen.

Marc Pachter discusses Lester's life at *Portrait of Invention: A Conversation with Lester Brown*, Smithsonian Museum of American History, June 18, 2009. *Photo by Hugh Talman.*

Ted Turner, Laura Turner Seydel, Lester, Rutherford Seydel, and Maureen at Ted's 70th birthday party, Atlanta, 2008.
Photo by Turner Enterprises, Inc.

Lester and Brian hiking in Denali National Park, Alaska, 2011.
Photo by Brian Brown.

Lester and Reah Janise getting
ready to run the Cherry Blossom
10-mile race, April 2005.

Brenda and family.
Back row: Lena, Chris, and Brenda.
Front row: Bridget, Cash, and dog
Carson, 2011. *Photo by Amii Harmon.*

Crossing the finish line of the Cherry Blossom 10-Mile
National Championship Race, Washington, DC, April 2008.
In 2009, Lester finished third in the 75–79 age group.
Photo by Marathon Photo.

Additional photos and historical documents can be found at
www.earth-policy.org/books/bng.

Another article that attracted wide attention was "Death in the Family Tree," by John Tuxill, which was featured in the September/October 1997 issue. His thesis was that humanity's continued population growth and expanding activities were threatening the survival of many of our closest evolutionary relatives. The 420 nonhuman species of primates, including chimpanzees and other apes as well as monkeys, are collectively among the most imperiled groups of mammals on the planet. The press conference, held in late August, drew a strong turnout, including seven television camera crews.

By 1990, when we had fifteen years behind us, we could say, as *The Wall Street Journal* had, that we were "wildly successful." We had fashioned a new model for public policy research institutes, one that relied on bright young generalists rather than those with specialized advanced academic credentials. And we were totally independent, accepting no government or corporate funding. And there was more to come.

9

Worldwatch: A World Leader

One Saturday morning as I was working at home, it occurred to me that with the stable of publications we had at that point—the *State of the World* reports, the Worldwatch Papers, and the magazine—we were accumulating a huge database of global trends. It also occurred to me that our individual researchers, who had been contributing chapters to the first half dozen or so *State of the World* reports on a particular topic, whether it was renewable energy, water, forests, food, or population, were acquiring enough information to write a book on each of these subjects.

Although we had written groundbreaking books throughout our first decade, when we started publishing *State of the World* with our small staff, we didn't have the time and resources to continue producing other books. We concentrated our energies instead on the new report. But now our research team had expanded to twelve and we had a broader institutional database to draw upon. Why not do a new series of books? To explore the idea, which came on a Saturday morning, I called one of my young colleagues, Alan Durning, who happened to live just a few blocks away, and invited him over for a mid-morning cup of coffee to discuss the book series. He was immediately responsive. And later when I broached the subject with the other senior researchers, it appealed to them too.

We decided to call them the Worldwatch/Norton Environmental books. During the 1990s we published twelve of these. Alan Durning wrote a book on overconsumption, *How Much Is Enough?* which became an immediate hit. Sandra Postel produced *Last Oasis*, a book that established her as a world authority on water. David Malin Roodman, barely thirty years old, produced *The Natural Wealth of Nations*, a book that made a convincing case for restructuring taxes by reducing income taxes and increasing taxes on environmentally destructive activities. Chris Bright, associate editor of the magazine, wrote *Life Out of Bounds*, the best book available on invasive species and the effect they are having throughout the world.

What was so amazing about our book publishing success at Worldwatch was that many of our books were written by first-time authors fresh out of school, more often than not with only a bachelor's degree. As *The Wall Street Journal* noted, we had become "a magnet for talent," hiring perhaps 1 out of every 300 applicants.

What I looked for in recruits was intelligence, judgment, and imagination. There are many very bright people, but not all of them have good judgment and still fewer are imaginative. We looked for young people who were either environmental science majors or who had majored in science, but who were also able to write.

For the institute, this was a period of rapid flowering and an extraordinary unfolding of talent. Each of these books was translated into several other languages, further strengthening

our efforts to supply the world with fresh environmental information. Several of the books won awards.

In 1991, as I was walking to work one morning, I had another
idea about how to make information on the environment even
more accessible: a short book of environmental indicators. Our
society was organized to provide huge amounts of economic
data on a daily or monthly basis. Newspapers were devot-
ing roughly two square inches each day to the prices of pork
bellies traded on the Chicago commodities market, posting
the day's high and low prices. Every month there were reports
on new housing starts, employment levels, and automobile
sales. But the world was simply not systematically tracking the
even more important environmental trends.

Was the earth's annual temperature rising or declining?
What about the world fish catch? How fast was wind-power
generation growing from year to year? What was happening
with world irrigated area? How were the earth's forests faring
in the face of unprecedented population growth? What was
happening with bicycle sales? And what about atmospheric
carbon dioxide levels?

There were many other data gaps, situations where the world
needed more data to make responsible decisions. As I was
thinking about the issues that morning on the way to work, I
was also thinking about the format, and I chose fertilizer use
as the one on which we could do a mock-up. Each indicator
would be allocated two pages: the left-hand page would be a
double column of text, a description and analysis of the trend
over the past year against the longer-term historical backdrop. The right-hand page would have a column of historical
trend data back to 1950 if they were available that far back. And
where appropriate, that column of figures could be accompanied by the trend in per capita terms to keep the focus on pop-

ulation. The upper right-hand side of the page would display a graph of the trend itself.

For the mock-up on fertilizer, for example, the primary graph was the world production of fertilizer from 1950 onward. A secondary graph compared fertilizer use trends in key countries like the United States, Russia, India, and China.

I took this mock-up to W. W. Norton, along with a list of the other indicators that could be included in the book. Like *State of the World*, this book would be produced annually. Iva Ashner, our contact person at Norton, was enthusiastic. The Surdna Foundation liked the idea and provided a substantial start-up grant.

On the staff, Hal Kane, Chris Flavin, Ed Ayres, and I took the lead. The first *Vital Signs*, which is what we titled this annual book series, was released in October 1992 at a well-attended press conference. Among the indicators it covered were world grain production, fertilizer use, carbon emissions, nuclear power generation, bicycle sales, automobile production, and growth of the world economy. When David Briscoe, environment reporter for the Associated Press, asked me after the press launch if he could take four additional copies for his colleagues, I knew we had another hit.

At this point, with a stable of publications that included two annuals—*State of the World* and *Vital Signs*—the topical Worldwatch/Norton books on environmental issues, the bimonthly *World Watch* magazine, and the ongoing Worldwatch Papers, we had a powerful lineup of publications with which to reach our global constituency.

State of the World continued to grow. In 1992 the first printing of the U.S. edition reached 100,000 copies. This did not include the English editions printed in the United Kingdom, India, and Australia. The German and Japanese editions, with first printings of 30,000 and 20,000 copies, respectively, followed the English edition. The Finnish edition of *State of the World 1991*, the first in that language, bounced immediately to the top of the best-seller list in Finland.

Just as we were reaching new highs, the United Nations was convening the 1992 Earth Summit in Rio. This two-week conference was the climax of a process begun in December 1989, with preparatory discussions and preliminary negotiations among the U.N. member countries. These led to the adoption of what was called *Agenda 21*, a wide-ranging blueprint for action to foster sustainable development worldwide. At its close, Maurice Strong, the conference secretary-general, called the Earth Summit a "historic moment for humanity."

Chris Flavin, Sandra Postel, and I had written the book *Saving the Planet* for the conference. As it turned out, we had the only book describing the challenges and potential goals of the Earth Summit. We held a day-long press briefing seminar that was organized and financed by our Worldwatch Norden affiliate, led by Øystein Dahle and Magnar Norderhaug. Ketil Gravir, a journalist with Norwegian Radio and a colleague of Magnar's, did an excellent job of moderating the session. Joining those of us on the staff—Chris Flavin, Sandra Postel, Hilary French, and me—were outside speakers Gro Harlem Brundtland, prime minister of Norway, who gave the opening address; General Olusegun Obasanjo, both a past and a future ruler of Nigeria; José Lutzenberger, former environment minister of Brazil; and Kazuo Aichi, former environment minister of Japan.

Interestingly, by the time the United Nations finally set the time of its opening session, it coincided with the scheduled Worldwatch press symposium. We were asked to change the time, but that was impossible, since the venue and the speakers had been lined up and the invitations sent out. As a result, we went ahead and held our press symposium at the same time as

the opening session. Over 170 reporters from 114 media organizations attended our event, far exceeding the number that
attended the conference's official opening. This suggested that
reporters were more interested in a serious discussion of the
issues than they were of the highly generalized, often overtly
political speeches by the national delegates. In addition to the
press symposium, my colleagues and I did roughly 100 media
interviews during the Earth Summit.

As a research institute working on global issues, we took
seriously the need to reach a global constituency with our
research results. For a small organization with a total staff of
thirty, this requires a lot of help. To begin with, we had to make
books a leading research product because book publishing is
the only segment of the communications media where there is
a well-established network of translators and publishers who
can move information into the world's leading languages.

A second pillar of the effort to reach this global audience
was a close working relationship with the communications
media worldwide. This included the wire services: Associated Press, Reuters, Bloomberg News, Kyodo News, Xinhua,
Deutsche Press Agency, Agence France Press, EFE News Service, Press Trust of India, and many smaller news agencies.
We also worked closely with national television and radio networks, including RAI in Italy, NHK in Japan, CCTV in China,
the leading U.S. national networks, and leading international
broadcasters like CNN, BBC, and Voice of America (VOA). The
latter two actually broadcast in many languages as they try to
reach a worldwide audience.

One thing we learned early on was the value of serving good
food at our press lunches. The institute became known not only
for its cutting-edge research, but also for its tasty food! Once
we made the investment in research, a small additional investment in a first-class caterer earned a huge return.

The great advantage of being located in Washington is that the international press corps is likely to be the best anywhere simply because this is where the political action is. It is an assignment to which reporters aspire. It is not only the U.S. government that attracts the press, but also the World Bank and the International Monetary Fund. It is thus a great place to have lunch with the reporters who are with leading news organizations.

By the mid-1990s, our clipping service was picking up forty stories per working day, and it covered only the more prominent newspapers and magazines in key countries. Our reputation and leadership in cutting-edge policy analysis translated into worldwide media attention. In essence, it meant that nothing we published was ignored. This is why Worldwatch became the most widely cited research institute in the world and why we often got a clean sweep of our releases by the big three electronic networks, the BBC, CNN, and VOA.

Early each year I went to Europe to launch *State of the World* in other languages. I regularly included Brussels, where Frank Schwalba-Hoth, a former German member of the European Parliament and longtime friend, would organize a briefing at the European Parliament. In 1992, I asked Frank for a personal favor, which was to help me find my ancestral village in southeastern Germany and my German cousins. The Berlin Wall had come down in 1989, and German reunification was finalized in October 1990. This was my first opportunity to find them. Three of the Schmidt (Smith) brothers had migrated to the United States in 1852. The fourth and youngest brother stayed in Germany to look after the parents. Two of his descendents also migrated to the United States, one in 1880 and another in 1922. My sister, Marion, the family genealogist, had located the village Frankenhausen in East Germany and actually had an address of the last known location of the German branch of our family.

I had been invited to speak at a conference in Berlin of the International Physicians for the Prevention of Nuclear War, a group that won the Nobel Peace Prize for their efforts on nuclear disarmament. Because of my scheduling constraints, I ended up speaking during the opening evening of the conference along with Willy Brandt, former chancellor and winner of the 1971 Nobel Peace Prize, with him leading off. After Brandt delivered his talk at the conference, I assumed he would leave, but much to my surprise he stayed to listen to me.

The president of the physician's group took Brandt and me to dinner in a small, private room in a nearby restaurant. I did not expect to be so impressed with Brandt, but it quickly became clear that I was in the presence of a person of strong character, one with distinctive leadership skills. Remembering the time Brandt had spent in Norway after fleeing Germany and potential arrest by the Nazis, I asked him whether he knew Gro Harlem Brundtland, three-time prime minister of Norway. He said that he did. Because her father was part of the Norwegian resistance to the Nazi occupation, they sometimes held meetings in the Brundtland home when Gro was a young girl running about the house. So Brandt said he had seen Gro but had not had much contact with her since then. (When I later mentioned to Gro the visits by Brandt to her home, she recalled them very clearly and realized that she had forgotten to mention them in her recently published autobiography.)

The next morning, Frank and I drove south toward Frankenhausen in Thüringen Province in an old Russian Lada, a car Frank had borrowed from Greenpeace. We arrived shortly after midday. When we went to the lone address we had, we learned from the woman living there that she did not know the family, but she did know that a woman who lived a few blocks away had been a childhood playmate of someone who had lived there. We located this woman. She directed us to someone else, who linked us to another potential contact, and so on. At 10 p.m., we established phone contact with my German cousin, Elke Gessner, and her husband Uwe. They were living in the town of Sangerhausen, seventeen miles northeast of Frankenhausen. We agreed to meet the next morning in the restaurant at the small hotel overlooking the charming village square in Frankenhausen where Frank and I were staying.

Frank and I are among the world's most casual dressers, but Elke and Uwe were dressed as though they were going to church, and while we were driving a decrepit Lada, they were driving a new Peugeot. Elke was a dental surgeon and Uwe an engineer. Clearly the poverty that permeated East Germany at this time did not affect everyone.

Initially they were suspicious, as anyone living in the repressiveness of East Germany had a right to be. But as we talked and exchanged information and looked at the photographs that someone had sent them a long time ago, it became clear that I was, indeed, their cousin. And, fortunately for me, they had a good command of English. We had coffee and talked for a couple of hours and then had lunch. Later, after visiting the local graveyard and touring the village area, we returned with them to their home in Sangerhausen for more coffee and some of Elke's homemade pastries before heading to the Berlin airport.

Since then, various members of our families have exchanged visits, including Marion and her husband Bob, Carl and his wife Mary Lou, and Carl's granddaughters, Leslie and Allison. In 1994, Elke and Uwe made their first trip to the United States to attend my sixtieth birthday party. My colleague Reah Janise had organized the surprise party, which was held in the grand ballroom of the Cosmos Club just a few blocks from our office. She had enlisted Scott McVay, head of the Geraldine R. Dodge Foundation, to use a ruse to get me to the event. She had invited people from all over the world. In attendance were Edgar Lin, from Taiwan; Prince Alfred von Liechtenstein; Bruce Babbitt, secretary of the interior; Eddie Albert, the actor; Jim Davis, my roommate from Rutgers; and lifelong friends Tom and Joanne Trail. My son and daughter, brother and sister and their spouses, and the guys with whom I'd played football for a quarter of a century also attended the party. And there were many more. I was in shock for the next few weeks.

Elke's daughter Christine was a medical student at that time, and my daughter Brenda had recently graduated from vet school. Not long after, Christine and her fiancé visited my daughter and her family at their ranch in Colorado and were excited to see that they do, indeed, have horses and that they use them to round up cattle, just like in the western films.

When I am doing a book launching in Berlin, Elke and Uwe meet me at the airport or train station and stay at the same hotel. They also usually sit in on my talks and press conferences, and I include them in dinners with German political leaders.

Our maternal grandfather's ancestry is the one branch of the family we have been able to trace back to Europe. Marion is still working on tracing the other three ancestral lines—Brown (English), Cain (Scottish), and Gallaher (Irish).

While all of my speaking invitations are interesting, a few stand out because they are what I referred to earlier as intersections with history. For instance, in 1990 I was asked to speak at Western New England College in Springfield, Massachusetts. My faculty host was Michael Meeropol. After I left campus, I learned that Michael was the elder son of Julius and Ethel Rosenberg. After his father and mother were executed as spies in 1953, he and his younger brother Robert were reared by the Meeropols. Michael, a member of the economics faculty, was a leader at the college in raising environmental awareness.

At about this same time, when I was in Frankfurt to launch the German edition of *State of the World*, our publisher, Fischer Verlag, organized a lunch for a half dozen people at a local restaurant. We were sitting there when the sixth member of the party arrived on a bicycle, parked it a few feet away—the restaurant was semioutdoor—and joined us. I thought my host had said that his name was Daniel Cohn-Bendit, the same as that of the French college student who had led the student demonstrations in Paris that culminated in the downfall of Charles de Gaulle. But that couldn't be, because Cohn was French and this was Frankfurt.

I said, "Are you Daniel Cohn-Bendit, Danny the Red [as he was labeled by the press]?" He said yes. He explained that he had since moved to Germany and been elected to the Frankfurt City Council. Later he became a German Green Party member of the European Parliament. Now he was referred to as Danny the Green. When I addressed the annual meeting of the European Green Party in Helsinki in 2006, *he* interviewed *me* for a video that was posted on the party's website.

Another time, while on a book tour for *State of the World 1991*, I was briefing President Mitterrand of France in his spacious office late one afternoon. During our discussion, one of the phones rang on his desk and a light started flashing. He glanced at the bank of phones and said, "I had better take that." So he went over and spoke for a half minute or so in French and then came back and sat down. He said, "It was Bush. I told him to call back in fifteen minutes."

The following day when reading the news I realized that the likely subject of their conversation was a joint communiqué they were working on in response to Saddam Hussein's refusal to let a U.N. team of nuclear weapons inspectors use helicopters in their inspections. The press reported the next day that Bush and Mitterrand said they would not stand by and let Hussein make a mockery of the United Nations.

Sometimes these intersections with history occur with Hollywood greats. In 1996, I was one of several honorary degree recipients at Villanova University, along with James Earl Jones. During a reception, when I asked him about his background, he said he had grown up in Michigan, living with his grandmother on her farm, and had enrolled at the University of Michigan as a premed student. But in his senior year, he realized, as many of us did at the time, that when he graduated there was a good chance he would be drafted and sent to Korea. Before that happened, he wanted to do something for fun, so he took a drama course. The world probably lost a good doctor.

Meanwhile, everything was expanding at Worldwatch. By the mid-1990s we had 159 book and magazine publishing contracts in some twenty-five languages. Of those, we bore the printing costs for only two, the English editions of the Worldwatch Papers and *World Watch* magazine.

One of the questions that I continually asked myself as the director of a research institute was whether our research products had any market value. People can always go to a funder and claim that their research products are valuable to society. But are they really? For me to comfortably make that argument, I first had to establish that we were producing products that people would buy.

From the institute's beginning, I sought ways to market our publications to cover as much of our budget as possible. In our first full year of operation, our earned income from publication sales, royalties, and honoraria totaled 8 percent of our operating budget. The next year, it climbed to 15 percent, then to new highs of 19 percent, 29 percent, 37 percent, and 46 percent. Then it climbed to over half, reaching 65 percent in 1992.

When I stepped down as president in 2000, I could look back at the institute's first twenty-six years, a span during which our earned income from royalties, sales, and speaking fees covered 51 percent of our expenditures. For most public policy research institutes this is more likely to be 2 to 5 percent. Worldwatch had done something that, as far as I know, no public policy research institute has done before or since: it had covered over half of its budget from the marketing of its research products.

In many respects, the evolution of Worldwatch was an institutional reflection of my personality. It included a commitment not only to research but also to the dissemination of research results, something that began for me with *Man, Land and Food* in 1963. Other personal traits reflected in the institute were the exclusive focus on systemic research and a strong commitment to efficiency. Among other things, my obsession with efficiency meant keeping the number of staff meetings to a minimum. It meant not publishing an annual report on the activities of the institute. And, as noted earlier, we did not need a budget officer. The leanness of the institute staffing was both admired and appreciated by funders. Bottom line: The entrepreneurial instincts that shaped the tomato-growing operation launched in my teens were the same that shaped the Worldwatch Institute.

Another source of the institute's efficiency was that in addition to being CEO, I was also a full-time researcher and did all the fund-raising. Reah Janise, who was both my assistant and vice president for special activities, also wore multiple hats, including managing our worldwide publishing network. Sharing my sense of efficiency, she is an expert scheduler, including my extensive travel itineraries. Whenever I needed extra help, such as transcribing an article or chapter over a weekend, I could always call on her.

As a manager, I requested regular reports on virtually every facet of our operation, including response to our direct mail promotions, earned income from publication sales, book royalties, subscriptions, honoraria, and interest earned on our operating reserves. Another indicator I followed closely was course adoptions in colleges and universities for *State of the World*. As the decade progressed, our other books such as *Saving the Planet, How Much Is Enough?, Last Oasis*, and *Who Will Feed China?* were also widely adopted for classroom use.

By the end of the century, we were firmly established as the world's most widely cited research institute. No other institute could remotely approach us partly because we had mobilized a vast array of book publishers and media outlets to disseminate the results of our research. Worldwatch had become the principal source of environmental analysis and information worldwide.

This is not to say that everyone was in agreement with our emphasis on environmental issues. Most of the criticism came from the far right. Two of my principal critics during the ODC and Worldwatch years were Herman Kahn at the Hudson Institute and Julian Simon at the Heritage Foundation. Both questioned the attention Worldwatch devoted to environmental destruction and resource depletion. They saw these problems as being solved with technology and market responses. Simon, an economist, argued in his book *The Ultimate Resource* that what the world needed was not family planning programs but more people. He saw people as "the ultimate resource."

Simon not only disagreed with what I wrote, but he was also apparently upset by the media coverage that my work generated. In a speech, he said that my views "run directly counter to the mainstream of agricultural economists. Yet he remains the most quoted writer on the subject. How come? How come Lester Brown and colleagues have the entire ear of the press and the nation?"

I never spent time responding to Simon's arguments. Kent McDougal of the *Los Angeles Times* wrote, "Although Simon's question was rhetorical, the answer seems to be that Worldwatch's products, packaging and promotion have a lot of appeal, especially to journalists."

The *State of the World* reports brought us many interesting visitors. In early 1997, the German Environment Ministry contacted us in Washington, indicating that the minister Angela Merkel would be coming to town and wanted to meet. I met with her late one afternoon at the Watergate Hotel. We had a great discussion, very informal and free-ranging, on world environmental issues, one that lasted for nearly two hours. She later did a book on the global environment in which she drew heavily on our discussion. Eight years later, she was Chancellor of Germany.

Merkel's political career has been meteoric and unique in many ways. For starters, she was from East Germany. She is also a woman, one with a PhD in physics. During her years as chancellor, so far totaling seven, she has been a strong leader not only in Germany but also at the international level, where she figures prominently in everything from shaping Europe's role in the world to the debate over how to manage the European currency crisis.

Meanwhile, I began to think about my personal timetable. In 1999, as I was reaching the common retirement age of sixty-five, I began to think about Worldwatch beyond me. One of the things that would enhance the institute's long-term prospects would be to create an endowment fund, but doing so would require a restructuring of the board, bringing on people with financial resources who could help.

As we moved in this direction, some new board members wanted more say in managing the institute than I was prepared to give. This board situation, combined with staff members who wanted to be more involved in decision making, coalesced into a move to replace me as president. At first I thought of fighting this move, but then at age sixty-six decided that it was not worth it.

Over the preceding years, I had occasionally asked myself whether the institute could survive my departure. I had wondered if I had created an organization that was so much a reflection of my interests, skills, and personality that it would be difficult for anyone else to sustain it as it then existed.

The prospect of no longer managing an organization in which I had invested twenty-six extraordinarily intense years was deeply depressing. But I also knew that I could not keep Worldwatch going forever. And I had promised myself early in my career that I would always be prepared to start over again if need be.

Worldwatch still exists, now under the able leadership of Robert Engelman, but on a much smaller scale, with fewer publications, most of which are written by outsiders. *World Watch* magazine no longer exists. And there are no longer any topical books being published.

The Worldwatch board proposed that I become its chairman and remain at the institute as a full-time research fellow. The latter had some appeal because I could devote myself fully to research and I would no longer carry the burden of management, staff recruiting, and fund-raising. Only having to think about my own research was a luxury I had not known for twenty-six years.

This arrangement was, however, only to last until early 2001, just a year or so. I had too many ideas—not only on research topics but also on new research products and ways of disseminating information. It was time to start a new organization. Reah Janise shared this thinking. We started to look for office space for what was to become the Earth Policy Institute. But before the story of that new institute, another one needs to be told.

10

The Food Debate with China

In 1994 I wrote an article for the September/October issue of *World Watch* magazine entitled "Who Will Feed China?" The late August press conference releasing it generated only moderate coverage. But when the article was reprinted that weekend on the front of the *Washington Post*'s Outlook section with the title "How China Could Starve the World," it unleashed a political firestorm in Beijing.

The response began on Monday morning with a press conference at the Chinese Ministry of Agriculture in which Deputy Minister Wan Baorui announced China's official disagreement with the analysis. He claimed that by 2025 they would nearly double their grain production and thus would have no trouble in satisfying their increasing food needs.

Although I was aware that the Chinese were sensitive to the notion that they might one day need to import large amounts of grain, I had not fully realized the depth of their sensitivity. Only thirty-three years had elapsed since the massive famine

in 1959–61 that came in the aftermath of the Great Leap Forward. The Great Leap was an ill-conceived national initiative
by Mao Tse-tung for China to industrialize quickly. It included,
for example, building hundreds of thousands of backyard fur-
naces to produce steel, none of which turned out to be usable.
So much labor was pulled from agriculture to build the fur-
naces and develop the coal and iron ore mines that the grain
harvest fell precipitously, leading to death by starvation of
some 36 million Chinese. The leaders in Beijing were survivors
of this massive man-made famine.

The national psyche of China clearly has been scarred by
this devastating famine in ways that we cannot even imagine.
The insecurity associated with potential dependence on the
outside world for part of their food supply was psychologically
difficult to accept. It was also politically anathema. In what
would become a common refrain, they said China had always
fed itself and it always would.

Then things quieted down until early November, when I was
in Tokyo to receive Japan's Blue Planet Prize. While there, Reuters correspondent Eiichiro Tokumoto asked if I could elab-
orate on my analysis of China's food prospect. We discussed
in more detail why China would likely become heavily dependent on the outside world for a large share of its food supply.
His story, carried on the Reuters world wire, was picked up
in China.

Shortly thereafter, an article appeared in the *China Daily*
written by Hu An'gang, a research fellow with the Chinese
Academy of Sciences in Beijing. Dismissing my analysis as
unbelievable and unscientific, Hu pointed quite proudly, and
rightly, to the dramatic gains made in grain production since
the birth of modern China in 1949. He accepted my projection
of the growth in future grain demand as population grew and

incomes climbed, but rejected my much less bullish outlook for grain production. His main point was that China had an enormous potential for expanding its grain harvest and that I was underestimating it.

What confounded the Chinese was that someone from outside China, who was not a China scholar, and who obviously had not seen much of Chinese agriculture, could make a projection of the sort that I was making. But my analysis and projections were not out of the blue. Several years earlier, I had noticed a pattern of changes in the grain supply-demand balance in countries that are densely populated before they industrialize. This had happened first in Japan and then shortly thereafter in both South Korea and Taiwan.

As industrialization accelerates, the demand for grain rises along with incomes. Grain production also initially begins to rise in response to the expanded market for farm products, but this increase is short-lived for two reasons. One, industrialization requires land—land for building factories, warehouses, and still more land to build the roads, highways, and parking lots that are hallmarks of a modern industrial economy. This loss of land leads to a steady shrinkage in cultivated area.

Second, as industrial wages rise, labor is pulled out of the countryside into the cities. In these densely populated countries, multiple cropping already had been pushed to the hilt in the quest for grain self-sufficiency. But this intensification requires a generous amount of labor in the countryside, enough workers to quickly harvest one crop and then prepare the seedbed and plant another. In countries of relatively small farms, the availability of rural labor was key to the extensive multiple cropping that existed at the time industrialization began. A loss of such crucial rural labor can prove catastrophic. Japan, for example, produced an average of 1.4 crops on every acre of cropland in 1960. Today, Japanese farmers average scarcely one crop per year. As demand climbs while production is falling, the dependence on imports soars.

In Japan, Taiwan, and South Korea, it was only a matter of time until each country was importing roughly 70 percent of its grain supply. All three were essentially self-sufficient in rice, their food staple. But they imported nearly all their wheat and also the corn for their rapidly growing livestock and poultry industries. I termed this sequence that leads from near self-sufficiency in grain to heavy dependence on imports in countries that are densely populated before they industrialize the "Japan syndrome."

It was almost inevitable that the same sequence would unfold in China. Although a much larger country, China still has a high population density, with roughly 1.2 billion of its 1.3 billion people living in the eastern and southern provinces that make up less than half of the country's geographic area. The rest of China, mostly mountains and deserts, is sparsely populated.

In 1988, I had sent a copy of my Worldwatch Paper *The Changing World Food Prospect* to Lin Zixin, the head of the Institute of Scientific and Technical Information of China and a longtime friend. Among other things, the paper discussed the Japan syndrome and its relevance for China. The purpose was to alert the leaders there to the potential for enormous growth in dependence on imported grain. But senior party leaders, preoccupied with making China an industrial power as quickly as possible, showed little interest.

After the economic reforms in 1978, the Chinese had restructured agriculture, shifting from large government-coordinated production teams to what was called "the household responsibility system," an approach that broke up the large collective land holdings, leasing parcels of land to individual families to farm. At the same time, the government strengthened its support for agriculture with a hefty rise in the procurement price for grain. These initiatives helped expand China's grain harvest by half between 1977 and 1984. It was a remarkable achievement—the result of adopting an enlightened agricultural policy.

But after this surge in production, Beijing relaxed its emphasis on the food front and began again to focus on industrialization. If China eventually imported most of its grain, following the path of its three smaller neighbors, it would put great pressure on the world's exportable grain supplies. While the world could meet 70 percent of the grain needs of a country like Japan with some 120 million people, supplying a similar share of food to one with 1.2 billion people would be a vastly greater challenge.

The *World Watch* article attracted more attention than anything I have ever written. In addition to appearing in our magazine's five language editions—English, Japanese, Chinese (Taiwan), German, and Italian—it also appeared in abridged form in many of the world's leading newspapers, including the *Washington Post*, *Los Angeles Times*, and the *International Herald Tribune*. It was syndicated internationally by both the *Los Angeles Times* and *The New York Times*. Among the other major news organizations covering the analysis were the Associated Press and *The Wall Street Journal*, including the Asian edition.

In early February 1995 I was in Oslo, Norway, to address an international conference of environment ministers, hosted by Prime Minister Gro Harlem Brundtland. The theme of the conference was sustainable development. In my presentation, I defined sustainable development—the process of meeting current needs without jeopardizing the prospects of future generations—and outlined a strategy for achieving it. In doing so, I illustrated some of the challenges that lay ahead on the food front by using China's likely emergence as a massive importer of food as a wake-up call that would force governments everywhere to address long-neglected issues, such as the need to stabilize population and invest more heavily in agriculture.

Following my presentation, we adjourned for a midafternoon coffee break and I left for the airport so that I could attend a dinner in Stockholm. Later I learned that when the session reconvened, the Chinese ambassador to Norway, Xie Zhenhua, asked for the floor even though he was not a scheduled speaker. He claimed that my analysis was misleading. The *Times of India* reported him saying, "We are giving priority to agricultural productivity. Our family planning program has been very successful. Science and technology and economic growth will see us through." In concluding, he repeated my question, "Who will feed China?" and then solemnly replied, "The Chinese people will feed themselves."

The following morning, Ambassador Xie, apparently bolstered by fresh information from Beijing, held a news conference pointing out "unequivocally that China does not want to rely on others to feed its people, and that it relies on itself to solve its own problems."

The Communist Party of China has a relatively small membership, one that includes scarcely 6 percent of the people, and thus cannot risk any major sources of instability, such as possible food shortages and the rising food prices that could come from a heavy dependence on imported food. This is why my projection of future growing dependence on imports was so unsettling in Beijing.

Yet even as my indirect dialogue with Chinese officials was taking place, the food situation was tightening within China. In late February and March of 1995, the tone of reports coming out of China began to change. On February 28, a Reuters story referred to the "sounding of alarm bells" by Communist

Party Chief and President Jiang Zemin and by Premier Li Peng about the state of China's agriculture. At the National People's Congress meeting in mid-March, officials acknowledged that "China is facing a looming grain crisis, with a hike in imports the only apparent solution to the demands of a growing population on a shrinking farmland." Extensive consideration of the food issue at the congress suggested that it was becoming a matter of concern within party circles.

Not too long after the meeting in Oslo there was a conference in Zurich focusing on the use of technology in dealing with issues such as food security. Both China's minister of science and technology, whom I had met earlier, and I were addressing the conference. He and his assistant used a good cop/bad cop approach. When speaking, the minister referred to me in discrete and positive ways in his talk, but when the floor was open for questions, his assistant, who was sitting in the audience, jumped up and loudly and aggressively challenged many of the basic points I had made.

The overall response to the magazine article suggested to me that it would be useful to do a more detailed analysis of China's agriculture. The result was the book *Who Will Feed China?* published in September 1995. The media coverage of it went viral. One of the most interesting responses was in Washington, DC, where the National Intelligence Council, the umbrella over all the U.S. intelligence agencies, analyzed the effect of China's growing demand for grain on world agriculture and any security threats that it might pose. A panel of prominent researchers, led by Michael McElroy, then head of the Department of Earth and Planetary Sciences at Harvard, produced a first-rate study of several hundred pages.

One of the team's conclusions was that China's cultivated area, according to satellite data, was actually substantially larger than officially reported. They said that although China could harvest more, the country nonetheless would be coming into the world market for massive quantities of grain in the not-too-distant future. They also recognized the effects of water shortages, soil erosion, and some of the world's most polluted air—all of which threatened China's agricultural prospect, essentially confirming my analysis.

Elsewhere, there were hundreds of conferences, symposia, and seminars on feeding China, only a few of which I could work into my schedule. One was organized by the Center for International Affairs at Harvard in early 1996. The two-day conference brought together a large group, including economists, foreign affairs analysts, agriculturalists, China scholars, and others. The event, entitled "Feeding China: Today and into the 21st Century" included among the speakers Michael McElroy, economist Jeffrey Sachs, and me.

Meanwhile, within China, every few weeks another study was released attempting to demonstrate why my analysis was wrong. These critiques came from such disparate sources as a scientist from the Chinese Academy of Sciences, an official from the Ministry of Agriculture, and an independent academic scholar. Not long after, an enterprising Chinese publisher took a copy of the original *World Watch* magazine article and a collection of the critiques of it and published them in a book entitled *The Great Debate Between Lester Brown and China*. The criticism of my work by the Chinese government did not bother me at all. Paradoxically, the more *Who Will Feed China?* was criticized in Beijing, the more it gained in credibility.

In early May 1995, I was invited to have dinner in Washington with Cheng Xu, director of science and technology in China's Ministry of Agriculture. He shared with me a thick folder containing a photocopy of my *World Watch* article and copies of a stack of articles responding to it, mostly in Chinese. Cheng said that the principal contribution of my article had been to focus the attention of China's leaders on agriculture, a sector they had been neglecting in the breakneck effort to industrialize. He was sharing these essays with me, he said, because he valued highly my intervention and the way in which it increased the resources available to those working on agriculture in China. Many Chinese officials working in agriculture saw the problems unfolding but were unable to do much to address them. In a sense, I had become their voice.

In commenting on my works, Jasper Becker, the Beijing bureau chief for the Hong Kong–based *South China Morning Post*, wrote that "[Brown's] arguments have caused near panic in the highest levels of the Communist Party and the government has responded by holding seminars and issuing defiant rebuttals. 'He has had a very big effect because grain is so important in China. It has forced the government to devote more investment to agriculture,' admitted Lei Xilu, an agronomist who works for . . . the State Planning Commission. In the past 40 years few other foreigners have managed to shake the confidence of China's rulers as Brown has."

Even as my analysis was being officially attacked and denounced, China was moving ahead aggressively on the agricultural front, launching an all-out effort to maintain grain self-sufficiency. The government quickly adopted several key production-boosting measures, including a 40 percent increase in the grain support price paid to farmers, a dramatic increase in agricultural credit, and heavy investment in plant breeding to develop higher-yielding strains of wheat, rice, and corn.

By far the most interesting encounter with official China came in April 1995 at a meeting of the InterAction Council, an organization whose membership consists exclusively of former heads of state. Founded in 1983 by Takeo Fukuda, formerly prime minister of Japan, and chaired by Helmut Schmidt, formerly chancellor of Germany, the council had always been frustrated because they had never had a former head of state from China since, until that time, all Chinese leaders had remained in office until their death. At the meeting scheduled for Tokyo, they invited, in lieu of a former leader, Huang Hua, who had been foreign minister and then vice premier from 1976 until 1992, when he retired at age seventy-nine.

This particular annual meeting of the InterAction Council was focusing on population, food, and development aid. They invited Nafis Sadik (head of the United Nations Population Fund), Robert McNamara (former president of the World Bank) as the authority on official development assistance, and me as the resource person on food. When I arrived at the meeting I learned that Huang Hua would be the discussant of my presentation. Even more interesting, he had brought with him copies of his response to the talk I had not yet given, which he proceeded to distribute to the members of the council as the meeting was beginning. It struck me as unusual, though flattering, that such a prominent retired political leader was brought into the fray to continue the Chinese challenge of my work and to assure all the former heads of state in attendance that China had always fed itself and always would.

We were all staying at the Prince Hotel in Tokyo and each day were bused to and from the hotel and the United Nations University conference center. Because of the tight security associated with the presence of so many former heads of state, the bus had a heavily armed military escort during our daily commute. On one of these rides, I sat next to Huang Hua, which gave me a chance to ask him some questions, such as where he was at the time of the Long March, the movement of people northward and westward who were fleeing the Chiang Kai-shek regime. He indicated that for a short time he was in Yan'an, the destination of the Communist marchers, and at one point was actually going out to meet the stragglers, many of whom were literally on their last legs, helping them into the camp.

Huang Hua had two sons—one a graduate of Harvard, the other of the University of Missouri. That night at a reception, I met the one educated in Missouri, who was now working in Hong Kong. When we exchanged business cards, I was shocked to see that he was working with Smith Barney, the U.S. investment firm. What a contrast: In one generation, the family had gone from the Long March to Smith Barney!

The following evening, a dinner cruise on Tokyo Bay, was even more interesting. Huang Hua's wife, He Liliang, a demographer by training, had asked earlier if we could sit together on the dinner cruise. I was surprised by her invitation, but agreed, eagerly anticipating the chance to talk with her. After we sat down in adjacent deck chairs, she—wearing a formal Chinese dress—opened her purse and pulled out a piece of paper folded many times over. It was a photocopy of the original "Who Will Feed China" article from *World Watch* magazine on which she had penciled notes in the margin in Chinese. For an hour or so, she went through the article paragraph by paragraph explaining "the errors" in my analysis. I began to feel like a character in a spy novel.

What I had not realized until I read Huang Hua's obituary after his death in November 2010 was what a key player he had been in China from the mid-1930s onward. He had attended an American missionary university in Beijing, where he had become proficient in English. When Edgar Snow wanted to interview Mao Tse-tung and his comrades in 1936, it was Huang Hua, then a secret member of the Communist Party of China (CPC), who went with Snow (who was one of Huang Hua's professors at the missionary university) to the hills in Shaanxi province, where Mao was located. Huang Hua was an interpreter for Snow as he gathered the material for writing *Red Star over China*, a classic on the Communist revolution then just getting underway.

During the revolution, Huang Hua became an assistant to one of the prominent Communist Party military leaders, Zhu De. When the CPC established the People's Republic of China in 1949, Huang Hua began work in the Ministry of Foreign Affairs, and among other things helped to negotiate the armistice that ended the Korean War. During the 1960s, he was ambassador to Ghana and Egypt. This was before he and his wife returned to China in 1969 and were sent to live and work in rural villages during the Cultural Revolution.

In July 1971, Huang Hua was assigned to meet secretly with Henry Kissinger in Beijing, a meeting that set the stage for President Richard Nixon's trip to China in February 1972. Huang Hua was centrally involved in arranging Nixon's visit to China and in reestablishing diplomatic relations with the United States. When China replaced Taiwan at the United Nations in 1971, Huang Hua became its first permanent representative to the international body.

In retrospect, I am awed to have had both Huang Hua and his wife involved in my own "reeducation" about Chinese agriculture. Among the few Chinese who were in the hills in Yan'an with Mao in the mid-1930s, Huang Hua was perhaps unique in that he served continuously in one increasingly responsible position after another into the early 1990s.

Over time, China's leaders came to both appreciate and acknowledge how *Who Will Feed China?* had helped change their thinking. A late 1998 issue of *Feedstuffs*, a weekly agribusiness newspaper, quotes Lu Mai, an agricultural economist and senior fellow at a government think tank in Beijing, as saying, "Brown seems to have been accorded guru status in high places. 'He's like the monk from outside who knows how to read the Bible.' "

When I later met Chinese Premier Wen Jiabao, in 2006, the first thing he said was, "Your book was very helpful to us." That same year, the National Library of China—the equivalent of the U.S. Library of Congress—gave the Chinese edition of my book *Plan B* (more on this in Chapter 11) its Wenjin Book Award. In 2003, Shanghai University honored me with an appointment as honorary professor. In 2005, the Chinese Academy of Sciences appointed me to an honorary professorship at its graduate school. In 2008, the China Institute of Water Resources and Hydropower Research followed with an honorary professorship in recognition of my work on world water issues, including those in China.

At this writing, China has emerged as a leading importer of grain. It also imports a staggering 60 percent of all soybeans entering world trade. Its grain and soybean imports are soaring—and there is no end to this rise in sight.

Thus the question "who will feed China?" is perhaps even more relevant today than it was in 1995. It is not so much a matter of population growth, because China's current population of 1.35 billion will be peaking at roughly 1.4 billion around 2027 and turning downward. Instead, the huge growth in the demand for grain in China is coming as its increasingly affluent society rapidly moves up the food chain, consuming more grain-intensive livestock, poultry, and farmed fish. The pressures of China's rising affluence on world food supplies are starting to show up in local village markets and at cash registers in supermarkets throughout the world.

11

Earth Policy Institute:
Time for Plan B

Reah Janise Kauffman and I began planning the Earth Policy Institute (EPI) in early 2001. And longtime friends Roger and Vicki Sant provided the half-million-dollar start-up grant, just as the Rockefeller Brothers Fund had done to launch Worldwatch twenty-seven years earlier. Janet Larsen (then my research assistant) and Millicent Johnson (manager of publication sales) also left Worldwatch, helping to form the core of our new organization. We were the first half of what would become an eight-person staff. Our purpose was clear: to provide a plan for moving the world off the decline-and-collapse path and onto a path that was environmentally sustainable.

The move from Worldwatch to our new office on Dupont Circle was scheduled for the first weekend in May 2001. Reah Janise and Millicent managed the process while I was tucked away in my apartment working on the institute's first book, *Eco-Economy: Building an Economy for the Earth.*

Although carpeting was a few weeks away and most of the

furniture was still en route, two days after moving in we held a press conference to announce the founding of this new environmental research institute. The reporters, who must have felt like they were literally present at the creation, were amused by the bare concrete floors. Then two weeks later we held another press conference to launch our first publication, a four-paged *Earth Policy Alert* on northwestern China's growing dust bowl and the dust storms that country was generating each year during late winter and early spring. When climatic conditions are just right, these vast storms can cross the Pacific intact, depositing dust across the western United States. Topsoil from China's northern plains is being exported—and at great cost.

Not wanting to lose any momentum, a week later we scheduled another press conference, this one responding to the Bush/Cheney energy plan, which was drafted in secret in consultation with the fossil-fuel industry. This new plan consisted almost entirely of building coal, nuclear, and natural gas–fired power plants. It did not even mention the word *wind*, even though wind power was the country's fastest-growing source of electricity generation, albeit from an admittedly small base. I was dismayed that the country that launched the modern wind industry was ceding leadership to Europe. C-SPAN covered our entire press conference on future sources of electricity, airing it several times over the next few weeks.

When *Eco-Economy* was ready for editing, we turned to Linda Starke, who had edited all of my books for nearly twenty years. It was shortly off to W. W. Norton & Company, and within a matter of weeks, the first printing of 40,000 copies was off the press.

On September 11, 2001, shortly before the book was released, I was scheduled to give a luncheon talk at the *New York Times*. I took the train to New York the evening before so I could have an early breakfast with Stirling Scruggs, a program director at the United Nations Population Fund, to discuss funding for the institute. Stirling's response was reassuring. I then headed back to my room in the Hilton Hotel at Fifty-Fourth Street and Sixth Avenue to work on another manuscript until lunch time.

Not long after, my daughter Brenda called from Colorado. She had first called the office in Washington only to discover with alarm that I was in New York. She then immediately called my hotel to see where I was and how I was doing. When I seemed confused by her call, she said, "Dad, turn on the television." I, like so many others, then watched the unfolding of the attack on the Twin Towers. Shortly after I tuned in, the south tower collapsed. We stayed on the line, Brenda listening on the radio in her pickup and I watching television, trying to grasp the meaning and scope of what was happening.

From my hotel window in the Hilton overlooking Sixth Avenue, I could see large numbers of people streaming north. The subway was closed. Offices had closed and were releasing their staffs. Hundreds of thousands of people were walking home.

Before lunchtime, I walked down to the office of the *Times*, then at 229 West Forty-Third Street near Broadway, to make absolutely sure that no one was expecting me. This was quickly confirmed. The paper was in scramble mode. I walked south on Broadway to get a closer look at where the Twin Towers had been.

It was difficult to comprehend. The early tally indicated the number of lives lost could be over 2,000. Television commentators such as Peter Jennings were likening it to the surprise attack on Pearl Harbor on December 7, 1941. The world changed on September 11, 2001. The public then learned about Al Qaeda, which was identified as the source of the attack. Later we learned the name of its head, Osama bin Laden.

In late afternoon, I called the University of Rhode Island, where I was scheduled to give the fall convocation address the following afternoon, to see whether it had been cancelled. They intended to proceed as scheduled. So the next step was to confirm that Amtrak would be operating. Miraculously, the 8 a.m. train on which I was booked was delayed only half an hour. As we departed and went under the East River and came up on the far side, I looked back at the Manhattan skyline. That's when the gravity of the attack really hit me.

Despite the events of the previous day, my convocation address went well and I was soon on the train back to Washington. Even though the luncheon talk at the *Times* did not materialize, *Eco-Economy* was enthusiastically received worldwide. Among the unsolicited responses was one from renowned biologist E. O. Wilson, who called the book "an instant classic." Shimon Peres, then deputy prime minister of Israel, said it was "a timely examination of an issue that needs to move to the forefront of the global agenda." And Børge Brende, formerly Norway's environment minister, said it was a "marvelous and inspiring book!"

Eco-Economy was translated into eighteen languages, some with multiple editions. In English, there were three editions: North America, India, and the United Kingdom and the other Commonwealth countries. There were two Chinese editions, one for the mainland and the other for Taiwan. In Spanish there was one for Spain and another for the Latin American market.

Given the enthusiastic worldwide reception of *Eco-Economy*, our first effort to give a sense of what an economy that was in harmony with the earth would look like, we felt we were on the right course. The world was hungry for solutions.

About this time I realized that devising a plan to reverse the trends undermining our economy was not a one-time event. It was an ongoing process, always adapting to advances in technology, policy breakthroughs, and the effects of mounting pressures on the earth's ecosystem. Keeping this plan current would fully occupy the energy of our staff of eight: five of us were researchers, and three handled outreach, sales, and administration.

While working on an updated version of the plan, I was having lunch with Catherine Cameron of the Wallace Global Fund. When I described what we were working on and asked if she had any ideas for a title, she said, perhaps because her foundation was an early promoter of Plan B, the morning-after contraceptive pill, "It sounds like Plan B to me." And so it was.

It has been clear to ecologists for some time that business as usual, which we call Plan A, is no longer a viable option. Civilization cannot survive the ongoing environmental trends of deforestation, overplowing, overgrazing, overpumping, overfishing, and overloading the atmosphere with carbon dioxide. It's a losing scenario.

Eco-Economy, the four subsequent *Plan B* books, and *World on the Edge* (2011) followed the same general model. The early part of each is devoted to identifying and describing the environmentally destructive trends that are undermining the economy and thus our future. The second half outlines Plan B—what it is going to take to reverse these trends.

Plan B has four components: stabilize population, eradicate poverty, cut carbon emissions 80 percent by 2020, and restore the economy's natural support systems, including forests, grasslands, croplands, and fisheries.

We wanted not only to present solutions but also to give a sense of the fiscal costs of doing so. The first *Plan B*, published in 2003, contained a budget for eradicating poverty and stabilizing population. Totaling $62 billion per year, it included the annual cost of achieving universal primary school education, basic health care, and access to reproductive health care and family planning services.

In *Plan B 2.0*, Janet Larsen, who is now our director of research and who knows more about most of the issues we work on than I do, developed an "earth restoration budget," which calculated the costs of such activities as reforestation, soil conservation, and setting aside marine parks to protect oceanic fisheries. The additional annual expenditures to protect the world economy's natural support systems totaled $93 billion. Combined with an upward revision in our social goals budget, we now needed an additional annual fiscal outlay of $161 billion.

With *Plan B 3.0*, the plan became both more comprehensive and ambitious. In deciding how much to cut carbon emissions to prevent climate change from spiraling out of control, we started with the science, not the politics. We did not ask what would be politically feasible. Rather we asked, How much and how fast do we need to cut carbon emissions to save the Greenland ice sheet and avoid an ultimate twenty-three-foot rise in sea level? Or how fast do we need to cut carbon emissions to save at least the larger glaciers in the Himalayas and on the Tibetan Plateau—the glaciers whose ice melt helps sustain the major rivers and irrigation systems of Asia during the dry season? This is why we concluded that the world had to cut carbon emissions 80 percent by 2020—not by 2050, as many political leaders have proposed.

Greenland is in a sense a metaphor for our global society. If we cannot cut carbon emissions fast enough to save the Greenland ice sheet, we probably cannot save civilization itself. If we reach the point where such a rise in sea level becomes unstoppable, it would alter not only how we think about the future, but, more fundamentally, what we think of ourselves. Reasons for cutting carbon emissions quickly are many, such as the threats posed by the crop-withering heat waves of the sort that decimated the Russian wheat harvest in 2010 and 2012 and the

U.S. corn harvest in 2012, but we need not go beyond ice melting to see that our civilization is in trouble on the climate front.

By the time we started thinking about *Plan B 3.0*, Jonathan Dorn, a first-class energy modeler, had joined the staff. He produced an energy model that enabled us to describe in detail how the world could cut carbon emissions 80 percent by 2020 through a combination of gains in the efficiency of energy use; shifts from fossil fuels to wind, solar, and geothermal energy; and an end to deforestation. Another colleague, Frances Moore, did the carbon modeling that enabled us to show how Plan B could halt the rise in atmospheric carbon dioxide levels at 400 parts per million by 2020. Once we reach this then we can focus on actually reducing carbon dioxide levels.

Having a detailed energy model did not greatly alter the budget for creating a sustainable civilization because Plan B had always depended largely on tax restructuring to create a low-carbon energy economy. The challenge was to raise the tax on carbon emissions, and offset it by lowering the tax on income. In effect, we can use tax policy in a revenue-neutral way to achieve environmental goals. Our thinking from the beginning was that if we could get the market to tell the truth—that is, to incorporate the indirect costs of burning fossil fuels, such as air pollution and climate change, into the prices of gasoline and coal-fired electricity—then the world energy economy would begin to restructure itself. The strategy is to create an honest market so that renewable sources of energy can quickly replace fossil fuels.

In *World on the Edge*, we noted that the newly estimated $185 billion of additional expenditures needed each year to eradicate poverty, stabilize population, and restore the economy's natural support systems—forests, soils, aquifers, and so on—could be done with a relatively small shift in defense expenditures. The $185 billion is less than a third of the U.S. defense budget. It is only an eighth of the global defense budget. We cannot say we do not have the resources to move the world economy off the decline-and-collapse path and onto one that can sustain progress.

One thing that helped me think about how we can make the needed changes in the world is what I call the three models of social change. One is the Pearl Harbor model, a situation where a catastrophic event changes everything. The second is the Berlin Wall model, where gradually building pressures reach a tipping point and suddenly lead to widespread social change, sometimes even a political revolution. The Berlin Wall coming down was a visual manifestation of a revolution that would change the form of every government in Eastern Europe. The Arab Spring in 2011 was a repeat of this mode of change as people took to the streets and overthrew autocratic repressive elements. The third model, which I call the sandwich model, is one where upwelling pressures for change among the population are matched by a desire for change at the top. This is the model that is now driving environmental progress in the United States. For example, the Sierra Club's grassroots-based Beyond Coal campaign is strengthened by the Environmental Protection Agency's enforcement of air pollution regulations on coal-fired power plants. As of early 2013, 142 of the country's 522 coal plants have recently closed or will close shortly.

We hope that our work at EPI can give ammunition to those working at the grassroots and to support policy initiatives for those at the top.

Whenever I have something new to say on an issue, I write it up as an article for a magazine or perhaps the *Washington Post*, *The New York Times*, or the *Guardian* in London, or we do a 1,200-word Plan B Update. We distribute these updates electronically not only to our worldwide list of editors, reporters, and bloggers but also to our house e-mail list and social networks. In addition, we hold a press teleconference to focus attention on a particular needed policy change.

For example, in 2006 EPI emerged as an early leader in opposing the use of grain to produce fuel for cars. We began with the release of an update entitled "Supermarkets and Service Stations Now Competing for Grain," noting that the amount of grain required to fill an SUV tank could feed one person for an entire year. Two articles quickly followed. The first I did, entitled "Appetite for Destruction," appeared in *Fortune* magazine in August. The other, "Starving the People to Feed the Cars," was carried in the Sunday Outlook section of the *Washington Post* and in twenty-one other newspapers. This was not a new worry for me. From the beginning of the ethanol-from-grain program in 1978, I was concerned about the potential effect on food prices. Indeed, in 1981, I wrote a Worldwatch Paper entitled *Food or Fuel: New Competition for the World's Cropland.* But it was not until Hurricane Katrina disrupted oil refining in the Gulf and the price of gasoline climbed to $3 a gallon that it became hugely profitable to invest in ethanol fuel distilleries. Indeed, the months following Katrina saw an orgy of these investments.

In early January 2007, we released an update that made it clear the biofuel industry was vastly understating the amount of grain that was being used to make ethanol. This exposé of the industry's systematic underreporting was needed because the U.S. Department of Agriculture was relying on the industry for data rather than tracking this burgeoning use of grain for fuel itself. We followed with an update entitled "Massive Diversion of U.S. Grain to Fuel Cars Is Raising World Food Prices." These releases generated hundreds of news articles, while some 160 websites either posted the food-versus-fuel updates or linked to them. I was called to testify about this issue on Capitol Hill before Senator Barbara Boxer and the Committee on Environment and Public Works in June 2007. The use of grain to fuel cars finally peaked in 2011 after six years of runaway growth and is now declining.

Another issue that EPI often weighs in on is bottled water, because its marketing is such a huge con job. Clever advertising is used to convince people that bottled water is somehow safer and tastes better than tap water. In reality, the regulations on the quality of tap water are generally much more stringent than those on bottled water. Bottled water costs 1,000 times as much as tap water yet it is often the same product—tap water—packaged and trucked from the bottling site to the consumer at an enormous energy cost. Janet has become a key resource person on this issue.

In June 2011, Janet did an update entitled "Cancer Now Leading Cause of Death in China." Typically, in the early stages of a country's development, the leading cause of death is infectious diseases. As countries develop, the mortality is caused more by the diseases of modernization, principally cardiovascular diseases. In China, which is in the middle stages of development, cancer rates have soared as a result of uncontrolled pollution. Given the fast-growing number of "cancer villages" and what we know about the lag time of exposure to pollutants and the onset of cancer, this situation is likely to get far worse.

We engage a wide range of environmental and environmentally related issues. For many years, I've been urging Japan, one of the most geothermally rich countries in the world, to harness that energy for power generation as so many other countries are doing. The standard response, which was nurtured by the nuclear lobby, was that tapping geothermal energy would mean disrupting their national parks because of the locations of their geothermal resources. In fact, geothermal energy is almost everywhere in Japan—and it's one of the world's cheapest, safest, and cleanest sources of electricity.

After the March 2011 accident at the Fukushima nuclear power plant in Japan following the earthquake and tsunami, we got the geothermal issue back on the table. Matt Roney, who tracks energy for us, did an update entitled "Time to Rethink Japan's Energy Future." He made a very basic point: Japan has a wealth of geothermal energy. With nearly 200 volcanoes and 28,000 hot springs, Japan has enough readily harnessable geothermal energy to back out all of its nuclear power plants. His calculations became a reference point for the media when discussing Japan's energy future. Now, at last, Japan has officially launched a program to harness its geothermal energy for power generation.

One of our challenges as an institute is how to help the world understand the resource constraints that we are facing in an ever-growing global economy, one where expectations are rising ever higher. We decided in 2005 to do an article that would look at what would happen to the demand for resources if China's income per person reached the 2005 level in the United States. At an 8 percent annual rate of economic growth, China would reach that level in 2031. In that future, if China were to follow U.S. consumption patterns with three cars for every four people, it would have over a billion cars—more than there are in the entire world today. It would consume more oil than the world produces. Its paper use would exceed that consumed by the world in 2005. In calculating China's consumption of these and various other resources, it became clear that the U.S. economic model is not a viable one for China. Nor will it work for the rest of the world, including the United States, for much longer.

Fewer than a dozen reporters attended the press conference we held for this update. For some reason, they were not inspired to write it up immediately. But that night William C. Mann, an Associated Press reporter who was probably on night duty, came across our release and wrote a story that was released at 2:43 a.m. By the time I got to the office that morning, the phone was ringing. One of the first calls came from the Russian equivalent of *The Wall Street Journal* in Moscow. Then came calls from Europe, including the *Financial Times* in London and the BBC World Service. Reporters were surprised by the calculation, but they also wondered how and why we were the ones uncovering this rather alarming projection. Unfortunately, the stir this piece created with its shocking calculations lasted only a short time before slowly fading off the radar screen. But the issue will not go away.

At EPI we try to anticipate and interpret emerging trends, such as the new geopolitics of food. For most of the last half-century, the overriding issue in international agricultural trade has been access to markets and how the United States, Canada, Australia, and Argentina could collectively pressure the Europeans and Japanese to open their markets. But as we moved into the new century, I concluded that the focus would soon shift to concern about access to supplies. As food supplies tightened in late 2007 and early 2008, and as grain prices soared to record levels, some countries began to restrict grain exports to try to keep domestic food prices under control. Russia and Argentina restricted wheat exports. Vietnam, the number two rice exporter, banned exports for several months as it tried desperately to keep its domestic food prices under control. Importing countries panicked.

Suddenly, these countries realized they could no longer depend on the world market to supply grain as needed. Their response was to try and buy or lease land in other countries to produce food to meet their import needs. By 2010, Saudi Arabia, China, South Korea, and others had acquired a total of 140 million acres, mostly in Africa but also some in Latin America and parts of Southeast Asia. This amount of land is equal to that planted in wheat and corn combined in the United States.

I summed up this analysis in an article entitled "The New Geopolitics of Food" in the May/June 2011 issue of *Foreign Policy*. It attracted more attention than any article I've written since "Who Will Feed China?" in 1994.

In it, I go behind the headlines on land grabs, noting that these are also frequently water grabs. Since it rarely rains in Egypt, for instance, its agriculture is entirely dependent on the flow of the Nile River. Sudan and Ethiopia, the two countries that occupy 70 percent of the Upper Nile Basin, are leading targets of land grabs by foreign governments and corporations. Millions of acres have been acquired. And much of the water to irrigate it will come from the upper Nile, which means less and less of the river flow will reach Egypt. In June 2011, I discussed this in an op-ed piece in *The New York Times* entitled "When the Nile Runs Dry."

Sensing the imminent stresses on the food front from these and related issues, I expanded the analysis into a book, *Full Planet, Empty Plates: The New Geopolitics of Food Scarcity*. It was released in September 2012. The main thesis is that the world is in transition from an era dominated by surpluses to one dominated by scarcity. The annual growth in demand for grain has doubled over the last decade, while constraints on production are making it more difficult for farmers to keep up. Some 3 billion people are moving up the food chain, consuming more grain-intensive livestock and poultry products. As a result, the world demand for grain is climbing at 41 million tons per year, up from 21 million tons a decade ago.

Usually I try to influence things by writing, but occasionally I get to talk directly with key decision makers. In early 2007

I had lunch with Shoichiro Toyoda, who headed Toyota when the company was emerging as the world's leading automobile manufacturer. We were first brought together by the World Expo near Nagoya in 2005, where he was honorary chairman and I served as an environmental adviser. At lunch, I lobbied him on the advantage of developing a plug-in Prius. I pointed out that in the United States we had a near-endless supply of wind energy, enough to run our economy, including powering our entire fleet of cars, many times over. We could run all of our cars on wind-generated electricity at a gasoline equivalent cost of 80¢ per gallon.

In a subsequent exchange of letters, I again pressed him on this point. It was always a good-natured back and forth, but he did take it seriously, and in a 2007 letter he said at the end simply, "Watch us." The plug-in Prius, which was test-marketed in the United States in 2011, was on the market in the spring of 2012.

In May of 2010, the University of Nagoya hosted an afternoon symposium on systemic thinking. On the symposium panel with me was Takeshi Uchiyamada, who spoke on the development of the Prius. In 1993 Toyota management had given Uchiyamada and his team of engineers the assignment of designing a car for the twenty-first century. End of instructions. Early on, they decided the car would have to be a hybrid, one with both an internal combustion engine and an electric motor.

The product of this exercise was the Prius. The third-generation Prius, which came on the market in 2010, can travel fifty miles on a gallon of gasoline. A remarkable piece of automotive engineering, it has set the standard for the industry worldwide. Takeshi Uchiyamada is one of my heroes.

Large investment banks, too, such as J.P. Morgan and HSBC, are interested in Plan B. This has led to numerous invitations for me to address investor conferences. In the Netherlands, Marcel de Berg, president of 21C, an investment management services company focused on sustainable and responsible investment strategies, decided in 2009 after reading *Plan B 3.0* that there was a need for an investment program guided by the Plan B goals. He was given strong public support by Herman Wijffels, the highly regarded former executive vice president of the World Bank. After more than a year of meetings and discussions, several of which I participated in, three large Dutch financial institutions—Rabobank, Robeco, and a pension fund for health care workers—came together in 2011 to create a Plan B investment facility. Collectively, these three firms have nearly $1 trillion in assets. They are now planning capital investments to build a Plan B economy, making the Netherlands the first country to do so.

After meeting with these firms in the fall of 2011, I flew to Zurich, where I'd been invited to talk with the Sustainable Asset Management team about a similar plan for Switzerland. As their name implies, they are already moving in the right direction.

More and more people are realizing the need to take climate change seriously. The recent spate of extreme weather events is driving some of this concern. During 2011, beginning in late March with an extremely active tornado season, followed by extensive flooding in the Mississippi basin, then heat, drought, and wildfires literally burning out of control in Texas, and then Hurricane Irene and Tropical Storm Lee, we saw the news channels become weather channels. Coverage of the destruction from tornadoes in Tuscaloosa, Alabama, and in Joplin, Missouri, went on for weeks, as did that of Hurricane Irene and the damage on the East Coast. A week after the hurricane, many who lost power remained without it. That fall, a surprise late-October snowstorm in the northeast dumped up to ten inches of snow in New York when leaves were still on the trees. Falling limbs left millions of people without power, some for up to two weeks.

Then came the Great Drought of 2012. The U.S. corn crop withered away, shrinking by 29 percent. This drove up food prices worldwide. As parts of the Mississippi River dried up, shipping was curtailed. Thousands of ranchers, with no grass and no feed, liquidated their herds. The secretary of agriculture prayed for rain, but his plea went unanswered.

Even as the heartland withered, late October 2012 brought Superstorm Sandy to the eastern United States. It was not a particularly strong hurricane when it hit, but it was huge, with a 1,000-mile wingspan. Instead of coming up the U.S. East Coast from the Caribbean and then moving in a northeasterly direction as storms typically do, the hurricane made an abrupt left turn—with the center of the storm coming inland across New Jersey.

The combination of the storm surge, the strong winds, and the heavy rain had a devastating effect in the middle Atlantic states, from Virginia through New Jersey and New York into Rhode Island. For the first time in recorded history, parts of southern Manhattan were under several feet of water. Seawater poured into the New York subway tunnels, leading to a closure of the system. Although the final figures are not in yet, it seems likely that Sandy will be by far the most destructive storm in U.S. history, exceeding the damage, for example, from Hurricane Katrina, which devastated New Orleans in 2005.

Just as the incident with Japan's Fukushima nuclear reactor altered the future of nuclear power, so too will more extreme weather events alter our thinking about burning fossil fuels. Carbon emissions are falling fast in the United States, the world's largest economy. We may soon reach a tipping point on the climate issue, much as we did with cigarette smoking beginning a generation or so ago.

In 2011, Germany got over 20 percent of its electricity from renewable sources; in 2012, it was roughly 23 percent. Electricity is now being generated from wind on a commercial scale in more than eighty countries. The cost of solar electricity is dropping fast worldwide. Cities around the world are carving out new bicycle lanes, introducing bike-share programs to encourage biking instead of driving. We are making progress!

As in earlier times and positions, I am still able to enjoy intersections with history. One came via a phone call from Roger Payne, one of the world's leading authorities on whales, in 2010. He was going to be in town and wanted to schedule lunch. I was eager to do so. In the late 1960s, Roger and researcher Scott McVay discovered and described the long, complex songs of Humpback whales at mating time and published a definitive cover article in *Science*.

A week or so later he called back and said he was also trying to have lunch with Maya Lin, who was going to be in Washington, but she could only do it on the day that he and I were planning lunch. He wondered if it would be okay if the three of us had lunch. I said by all means. This was an unexpected opportunity to sit down with two people I had long admired.

During lunch, I asked Maya how long it had taken her to come up with the concept for the Vietnam War Memorial once she visited the site. She said it took only three or four hours. It was one of those things that came almost immediately. She then took her initial visualization and translated it into the winning design. There were 1,442 designs submitted in the competition, all anonymously by number. Maya had concluded, I later learned, that if it were known that she was of Asian extraction, a female, and a student (at Yale), she could not possibly have won.

New experiences do not come often to someone who has been around as long as I have, but they do still occur. In March 2012, we received a handwritten letter with a check for half a million dollars. It was from Henry Ingwersen, a ninety-year-old retired Air Force Colonel. Like us, he was concerned about the future of civilization. He said he didn't know if the world could be saved, but if anyone could do it, he thought it would be us. He had sent us his life savings.

Another once-in-a-lifetime experience came in October of 2012 when Reah Janise put a copy of *Plan B 3.0* in Esperanto on my desk. For the younger among us, Esperanto is a language that was created to become the world's lingua franca. But even as Esperanto was being promoted, English was taking over as the common language that tied the world together.

I was surprised because I'd forgotten we had signed a contract with Robin Beteau in cooperation with Eldona Fako Kooperativa. Although I've been published in over forty languages, until this, Basque was perhaps the most exotic language in which I'd been published. But Esperanto? Who would have guessed!

As I look back over the twelve years since starting EPI at retirement age, it was clearly the right decision. The combination of being freed of the management responsibilities of a large organization and having such a talented support team here at EPI has enabled me to focus on making these years among the most productive and satisfying ones in the half century I have been in Washington. And, no, I am not yet done.

12

Reaching the World

I have faced two great challenges in my career. One was fashioning Plan B. The other is the ongoing campaign to convince the world to adopt it.

Moving civilization off the decline-and-collapse path requires a mobilization at the global level comparable to that of the United States during World War II. In 1942, the United States totally restructured its industrial economy, shifting production from cars to planes and tanks. This restructuring did not take decades or even years. It was done in a matter of months. Today, we need to restructure the world energy economy with a similar sense of urgency if we are to stabilize climate.

Our effort to get the world to adopt Plan B, or something very similar to it, begins with book publishing since, as noted earlier, this is the only segment of the information economy with a well-developed translations capacity. Our publishing network is anchored by W. W. Norton & Company in New York. My publishing relationship with Norton began in 1974 when they published *In the Human Interest*, the background book for the World Population Conference held in Bucharest. Since then, they have published the English edition of each of the forty-nine books, including seventeen *State of the World* reports, that I have authored or coauthored. Norton, which has a strong U.S. marketing presence both in bookstores and on college campuses, is an ideal publisher for me—a marriage made in heaven.

The understanding with W. W. Norton is that they will publish everything we send them and that we will send them everything we do. Our contact person, Amy Cherry, who is vice president and senior editor, is a sheer delight to work with.

Our worldwide book publishing network, so essential to our success, has been built one publisher at a time. It took years to put it together, but it all began in 1963 with *Man, Land and Food*, which appeared in French and Spanish. I continued building from there, eventually publishing in some forty-three languages.

One of our long-standing publishing arrangements is with Earthscan, the first environmental book publisher in the United Kingdom. Here, Jonathan Sinclair Wilson was our contact, taking responsibility for marketing our books in the Commonwealth countries as well. My relationship with Jonathan covers thirty books.

Our Italian publishing arrangement goes back nearly thirty-five years. In 1978, a young Italian environmentalist, Gianfranco Bologna, offered to translate *The Twenty Ninth Day*. He then arranged for its publication. When we finish a book, we send an early copy to Gianfranco. He then assumes responsibility for finding a publisher, which for many years has been Edizioni Ambiente. Thanks to Gianfranco, who is now scientific director of WWF Italy, thirty-one of my books are available in Italian.

Another of our long-standing publishing relationships is with China. When I first met Lin Zixin in 1981, he was the head of the Institute for Scientific and Technical Information of China, a government organization whose purpose was to scour the world's scientific literature looking for articles that should be translated into Chinese and distributed to scientists, academics, and party leaders.

It was in this context that Lin discovered Worldwatch and published *State of the World 1984*, the first in the annual series, in Chinese. His son, Wei Lin, a professor of civil engineering at North Dakota State University, often serves as our go-between. Despite our contrasting political and cultural backgrounds, Mr. Lin (which is what I call him) and I are bound by a shared view of what is happening to the earth and what needs to be done to remedy it. I refer to him as my Chinese brother. Some twenty-nine of my books have appeared in Chinese, including, after some delay, *Who Will Feed China?*

In Japan, *State of the World 1984* was initially released by an agricultural publishing house. Soki Oda, the editor, was convinced that the book had to be published in Japanese. It was a hit. Eventually he assumed responsibility for getting our books published in Japan and also for organizing highly successful book launchings. Frequent appearances on Japanese television led to an invitation to moderate *Voyage to the Future*, an environmental documentary that aired on NHK, the national broadcasting service. Thanks largely to Soki, forty-five of my books have appeared in Japanese, making it second only to English.

Junko Edahiro, who initially both interpreted and translated for me, is another extraordinarily helpful contact in

Japan. A force of nature, Junko started her own NGO, Japan for Sustainability, and another consulting firm on the benefits of using systemic thinking in policymaking and planning. She has also written several books, including *Anything Is Possible if You Wake Up at 2 A.M.* In 2004 she was chosen as Japan's most successful career woman by *Nikkei Career Women* magazine.

Meanwhile, from another corner of the world, Magnar Norderhaug, who worked for the Norwegian aid agency, visited me in Washington in 1989, indicating an interest in publishing *State of the World* in the Nordic languages. Working with Øystein Dahle, former vice president of Exxon for Norway and the North Sea, and Ketii Gravir, a Norwegian journalist, he formed Worldwatch Norden to facilitate publication of the *State of the World* reports in Norwegian, Swedish, Finnish, and Danish. From 1990 onward, each year in late January, I would devote an intense week to launching the Nordic editions, accompanied by Magnar. It was a remarkable tribute to Magnar that he could not only get these books published in these countries, but he would have them all translated and ready for release within a month of the U.S. edition.

In 1987, I was contacted by Ion Iliescu, who was associated with a Romanian publishing house, Editura Tehnica, and was interested in doing *State of the World*. Iliescu wrote a twenty-three-page introduction to the first Romanian edition, relating the global issues to those of Romania.

After the ouster of the dictator Nicolae Ceaușescu during Christmas week of 1989, Iliescu became the leader in setting up a democracy. Two years later he became the first elected president of Romania, serving two four-year terms. President Iliescu still writes the Foreword for each of my books in Romanian. Now in political retirement, he personally organizes the launchings himself. When I cannot make it to Romania, he launches the books as though they were his own. With our many shared concerns and twenty-five years of working together, we have developed a lasting friendship.

Shortly after the contact from Iliescu, we received a letter from Hamid Taravati, an Iranian doctor who had picked up the English edition of *State of the World 1989* in a bookshop near Tehran University. He found the analysis so engaging that he began translating it that same day. He had found practicing medicine alone to be unsatisfying, given the overarching environmental challenges his country and the world were facing. He wanted to do something more.

He asked for the rights in Farsi, which we readily granted. Hamid and his wife, Farzaneh Bahar, also a doctor, have worked hard to translate and publish our books in Iran. It is not unusual for an individual Iranian government ministry to bulk purchase 500, 700, or even 1,000 of the Farsi editions. In a country where independent research is rare, my books are highly valued, particularly in government ministries and universities.

Two books, *Full House* and *Eco-Economy*, won literary awards in Iran. The first was from the Ministry of Culture, the other from the Peka Institute, an Iranian publishers association. Both awards attest to the translation skills of Hamid and Farzaneh. Ironically, although the United States and Iran do not have diplomatic relations, the publications of a small research institute on Think Tank Row in Washington, DC, appear to be the leading source of global environmental information for Iranians.

Meanwhile, in South Korea in the 1980s, the young man who was to become our publishing contact person languished in jail for six years. A leader of the democratization movement in South Korea at that time, Yul Choi's goal was to unseat President Park and replace him with a democratically elected president.

While in prison, Choi read many books, including one of mine. He vowed that if the democratization movement succeeded, he would then divert the movement's energies to saving the environment. This led to the creation of the Korean Federation Environment Movement. The most effective environmental organization in Asia, with 85,000 members and forty-seven local branches, it now arranges for the Korean editions of our books. For his incredible work, Yul Choi was awarded the Goldman Environmental Prize in 1995.

In Turkey, EPI's partner is an NGO with the acronym TEMA, an organization dedicated to reforestation and soil conservation. The organization has two founders: Nihat Gökyiğit, a highly successful businessman, and Hayrettin Karaca, a prominent academic. In addition to launching a massive tree-planting effort in Turkey, they also saw the value of publishing our books. When I was on a book tour visiting Istanbul and Ankara in 2008, I visited TEMA's office in Istanbul. They asked me to autograph their library copy of each of the sixteen books of mine that they had published in Turkish.

While many of our publishing relationships go back two or three decades, there are also promising new ones. For example, Lars and Doris Almström, two university professors in Sweden, asked permission to translate *Plan B 2.0* and make it available online. We granted them the rights to do so. When they were translating the next book, *Plan B 3.0*, they found a publisher and organized a first-rate launch in Stockholm. Both then took early retirement so they could focus on promoting the adoption of Plan B in Sweden. They have now published four of our books in Swedish and are actively working to implement Plan B. Doris's effort recently earned her two environmental awards.

In 2006, we received an e-mail from Pierre-Yves Longaretti, one of France's leading astrophysicists and the codirector of Laboratoire d'Astrophysique de l'Observatoire de Grenoble.

Pierre-Yves realized that his work, however cutting-edge in astrophysics it might be, was not responding to the imminent threats to our earthly future. After picking up *Plan B 2.0*, while attending an astrophysics meeting in California, he sought our permission to translate and publish it in France. Pierre-Yves worked nights, weekends, and during vacation to translate the book into French himself. His close friend, Philippe Vieille, who shared his concerns, edited it. The French edition of *Plan B 2.0* was launched in Paris by Calmann-Lévy, one of France's premier publishing houses, in coproduction with Vieille's publishing house Souffle Court Éditions, in November 2007.

Pierre-Yves and Philippe have started a nonprofit organization, Alternative Planetaire, to implement Plan B in France. They released *World on the Edge* in French in conjunction with publisher Rue de l'Echiquier, and they are publishing *Full Planet, Empty Plates*.

Sometimes, where book markets are small, we grant the rights to individuals to translate and then either upload the electronic edition to their website or upload it on ours. Such is the case in Hungary, where David Biro, a schoolteacher, has been doggedly translating our books, beginning with *Plan B 3.0*. He's now working full-steam on *Full Planet, Empty Plates*. In Greece, Makis Fountoulis published *World on the Edge* by getting sponsors. He is looking to do the same with *Full Planet, Empty Plates*.

In Latin America, we work closely with Gilberto Rincon of the Center of Studies for Sustainable Development in Colombia. He has arranged for the Spanish editions of my last five books, including *Full Planet, Empty Plates*. Gilberto also organizes large international conferences built around the book launchings.

Reinforcing the translation and distribution of the books themselves are documentaries based on them. For example, as noted in Chapter 8, the early editions of *State of the World* inspired a ten-part series, *Race to Save the Planet*, that ran nationally on PBS in fall 1990 and soon thereafter in other countries. In 1999, a coalition that included NHK of Japan, CNN, and a consortium of European television networks produced a six-part series entitled *State of the World*, which aired in 2000. And in 2003, NHK aired a two-hour, two-part program entitled *Voyage to the Future*, mentioned earlier. I moderated the second hour, which was subtitled *Eco-Lessons with Lester Brown*. And in December 2008, NHK did *Save the Future*, a ninety-minute program based entirely on an interview with me that ran as a New Year's Day feature in 2009.

The most recent film, *Plan B: Mobilizing to Save Civilization*, narrated by Matt Damon, appeared in the PBS *Journey to Planet Earth* series. Brilliantly produced by Marilyn and Hal Weiner, it first aired nationally on PBS in March 2011. At the suggestion of Joan Murray of the Wallace Genetic Foundation, Marilyn and Hal accompanied me on a 2008 book tour to launch the Japanese, Korean, Chinese, Hindi, Turkish, and Italian editions of *Plan B 2.0*. They captured some of my interactions with the media and political leaders, which gave the film a strong global ambience. In addition to running several times on PBS, the film is now running on networks in other countries.

There is also a network of individuals who personally distribute copies of our books. When we started publishing the *Plan B* series, we noticed from our sales database that people were ordering multiple copies from us for distribution to friends, colleagues, or opinion leaders. We decided to recognize the people who bought five or more copies of *Plan B*, calling them the Plan B Team. We have now expanded this to include the more recent books, *World on the Edge* and *Full Planet, Empty Plates*.

As of 2013, the team has over 4,000 members and counting. We designated Ted Turner captain of the Plan B Team because he typically distributes some 4,500 copies of each book to world leaders, including members of the U.S. Congress, the European Parliament, state governors, university presidents, Fortune 500 CEOs, heads of state, cabinet leaders, heads of leading environmental NGOs, and most of the world's 500 or so other billionaires. Ted not only distributes these books, but he also sends a letter to each book recipient saying, essentially, I've read this book, it's important, and you should read it too.

I do not know anyone who is more committed to saving the environment than Ted. He not only preaches it, he practices it. It permeates everything he does. When he acquired 2 million acres of land in the United States, mostly rangeland, he became the country's largest landowner. On his fifteen ranches in Colorado, Kansas, Montana, Nebraska, New Mexico, Oklahoma, and South Dakota, he has helped return the land to its natural state. All told, he now has more than 55,000 bison grazing on his ranches—without fences or buildings. Ted notes with pride that the amount of organic matter in the soil has increased markedly, sequestering huge amounts of carbon. Spending time with Ted on one of his ranches, as my partner Maureen Kuwano Hinkle and I have done, is an uplifting experience.

The Turner book distribution model has been adopted in Japan, where the Kurosawa brothers, Toshishige and Masatsugu, distribute thousands of copies of each book to Japanese opinion leaders, including members of the Diet and corporate leaders. In Turkey, TEMA arranged a complimentary distribution of an astonishing 4,250 copies of the Turkish edition of *Plan B 3.0* to political and opinion leaders.

Building this global network of book publishers has been a deeply rewarding experience. There is no other network quite like it. In addition to publishing in all the major languages, we also occasionally appear in minor ones such as Basque, Georgian, and Estonian. Having so many people pushing so hard to change the world boosts the morale of all of us at EPI. We cannot afford to slow down.

As a result of the efforts of literally hundreds of translators, editors, and publishers, some 658 editions of my books have appeared in various languages. But while reaching large numbers of people depends heavily on the written word, reaching concentrated groups of key decision makers depends on public speaking—addressing conferences of political leaders, corporate leaders, investment bankers, professional societies, and many others. In trying to convince people that we need to restructure the world economy, and thus move the world back onto a sustainable path, I have given 1,863 talks in forty-seven countries over the last half century. Sometimes on an international tour there is just a single stop in the capital, such as London, where the U.K. newspapers and other media are concentrated. In France, Paris is the key. In Italy, however, a book tour may involve Rome, Turin, and Milan. In China, which like the United States has both a political and a financial capital, the key cities are Beijing and Shanghai. In Japan, Tokyo will usually suffice.

Press conferences help to develop media contacts; meetings with individual reporters help build and reinforce media relationships. Over the years I have had literally thousands of lunches, breakfasts, and dinners with reporters.

Few accomplishments are more satisfying than fully engaging an audience. This is why actors act and singers sing. It is why I speak. Linton Weeks, who profiled me for the *Washington Post* a few years ago, accompanied me to a talk to some 700 defense contractors meeting at the Marriott Wardman Park Hotel in Washington, DC. In the profile, he wrote that the audience became so quiet "you could hear the ice melt."

Each year Frank Schwalba-Hoth, a former German Green Party member of the European Parliament, organizes a talk for me at the Parliament in Brussels, one that is open to the public. Frank does such a great job that this gathering now requires advanced registration to avoid overcrowding the lecture hall. The range of groups I have recently addressed include the annual conference of the European Green Party in Helsinki, the International Parliamentarians' Conference on Population and Development in Bangkok, and the Chinese People's Congress 21st Century Forum in Beijing.

It is essential to reach business and financial leaders, such as those who gather early each year at the World Economic Forum in Davos and at the triennial World Energy Congress. Investment groups I have addressed range from J.P. Morgan in New York to HSBC in London. Other public lectures are sponsored by leading corporations with their own impressive outreach capacity, such as the Coca-Cola lecture in Tokyo or Google's lecture series at its headquarters in Mountain View, California.

Beyond the business community, professional associations loom large in my speaking schedule. These include keynote addresses at such conferences as the International Congress on Environmental Law in Bogota, the World Conference on Disaster Management in Toronto, and the International Forum on Food and Nutrition in Milan. Religious groups range from the annual conference of U.S. Quakers to the Central Conference of American Rabbis.

The 262 lectures I have given at 153 colleges and universities in sixteen countries also help to reach potentially large audiences. The three universities that I have lectured at most frequently are Harvard (13), Columbia University (10), and the University of Tokyo (9). More and more universities are launching annual environmental lectures in their efforts to give the issue the attention it deserves. Among the schools where I had the honor of inaugurating these series are the University of

California–Berkeley, Oxford University, and most recently the University of Maryland.

In addition to the actual appearances on campuses, many schools, such as the University of Colorado, post lectures on YouTube. Occasionally a lecture shows up on C-SPAN, such as one I gave at the University of Chicago.

YouTube provides a welcome audience for talks. At this writing there are excerpts on YouTube from some sixty talks and interviews I've given in countries from Brazil to Sweden. Interestingly, while the actual attendance at the talks is typically numbered in the hundreds, YouTube viewings number in the thousands. For example, the talk I gave at the University of California–Berkeley's Distinguished Lecture Series has been viewed 14,146 times. A talk to an audience of nearly a thousand in Mexico City has been viewed 39,313 times on YouTube. These Internet multipliers are hugely helpful in disseminating our research findings.

Aside from press conferences, the most efficient way of getting the word out is through interviews with individual reporters. How many interviews have I done? I've never counted. But if I have given 1,800 talks, the number of interviews goes into the thousands. When on an international book tour, my daily schedule often includes eight or ten interviews in a day. These consume time, but they enable reporters to focus on issues that are of particular interest to their readers, listeners, or viewers.

Many interviews are spawned by press conferences when individual reporters want to follow up with more specific, more detailed questions. Occasionally my host publisher will organize a press conference in the airport when I arrive, as was the case not long ago in Istanbul. And sometimes a reporter will ride with me to the airport, to squeeze an interview into my already full schedule, as recently happened in Tokyo.

The traditional press conference of gathering people

together in a room, which worked so well at Worldwatch with press lunches, is being replaced in some countries by press teleconferences. These usually involve a presentation of fifteen to thirty minutes and then questions and answers from reporters for up to half an hour.

The topics covered in my talks and interviews vary widely, but one issue that comes up again and again is population growth. During the early 1950s and 1960s, an early generation of demographers analyzed the relationship between population growth and the earth's resources, but with time demographic research shifted to the nitty-gritty of demographics. As demographers turned inward, the media turned to natural scientists for commentary on population growth and its effect on the demand for resources, the environment, or food security. Biologist Paul Ehrlich and I have been center stage in trying to keep focus on the broader implications of growing human numbers. Paul published *The Population Bomb* in 1968, a book that was explosive in its own right. He is exceptionally articulate, an excellent interviewee. My visibility on the issue dates back to the publication of *Man, Land and Food* in 1963. For me it is impossible to write about food, water, or climate change without incorporating the effect of population growth. When world population reached 7 billion in October 2011, the media turned to both Paul and me for commentary. This was not surprising, given that both of us have been tracking this issue for half a century and have seen world population triple during our lifetimes.

It is rare for me today to give a talk at an international conference without at least a few people coming up afterward to say something like, "Thank you for your work. I've been reading you for years." Or "I've been reading you since the first *State of the World.*"

For instance, in May 2008 I was scheduled to meet Justin Fox, a reporter with *Time*, for lunch at the Oyster Bar in New York's Grand Central Station, but as I was walking east on Forty-Second Street, I couldn't decide which entrance to take to reach the restaurant. When I asked a passerby for guidance, he said he thought it was the next one. When we reached it, he said, "Let me just show you where the Oyster Bar is." When we got within sight of the restaurant, he started to peel off. As he did, I thanked him and handed him my business card. He stopped, stared at it intently, and then looked up and said, "I've been reading you for a hundred years!" It turns out that he, Alexander Peters, is a prominent player in the New York real estate market. But that is his day job. He is also on the Board of the Long Island League of Conservation Voters, which was why he had been reading me for "a hundred years."

13

Reflections

We are a product of our times. For me, the son of a dirt farmer, born during the Depression, acquiring a work ethic came early—well before I started school. More broadly, my own work, indeed my life over the last half century, has been shaped by the realization that it is my generation that has moved the world onto an economic path that is not environmentally sustainable, a path that has us headed for decline and collapse. The challenge of reversing this process has shaped my life.

Although I grew up in a family that was far from affluent, it was remarkably stable. In this social environment, expectations were low. If your parents had not graduated from elementary school and never traveled much beyond the local community, they were not so likely to press you on the educational front. This lack of high expectations provided a wonderfully pressure-free environment that let me set my own goals.

Being steeped in the biographies of historical figures in

my youth led me to identify with people who attempted and achieved seemingly impossible goals. The subjects of these biographies were responding to the great issues of their time. For Galileo, it was showing that the earth revolved around the sun, not the other way around. For the founding fathers, it was achieving independence and building a new country, one with a democratic form of government.

Although I had launched a promising farming operation during the 1950s with my brother Carl, by the summer of 1958 my mind was already turning to some of the larger issues facing humanity. The months spent living in the villages of India when I was twenty-two certainly reinforced this interest. It also helps explain my early attention to world population growth, soil erosion, and hunger. Once you understand the effect of soil erosion on the sustainability of agriculture, it is a short mental step to see how environmental trends more broadly threaten the sustainability of the global economy and, indeed, of civilization itself.

Looking back, it is clear that I have been the beneficiary of both a strong public educational system and a society of unmatched social mobility. Where else could one be the first in a family to graduate from elementary school and later be recognized with a stack of honorary degrees?

In retrospect, I realize that at every stage of my life I've been able to shape my own agenda. When I was in grade school, my overriding interest was in learning, which went far beyond our classroom assignments. Learning was also reading books.

Starting a tomato-growing business while in high school was also a learning experience, one that helped me to find my strengths. More specifically, I learned how to borrow money, to recruit workers, to manage, and to use time efficiently.

When I joined the Foreign Agricultural Service at the USDA, my official assignment was the Rice Bowl countries, but my real interest was the world. I wanted to get to know world agriculture and know it better than anyone. Continually raising the bar on what I wanted to do helped me to discover what I could do.

Having grown up on a farm and farmed myself for eight years, I look at the world through the eyes of a farmer. Systemic thinking comes naturally to farmers, who necessarily have to deal with a wide range of issues. As a farmer you develop an understanding of nature as it relates to agriculture in all its complexity. For example, during a full moon, tomatoes ripen faster, requiring more baskets and pickers, than during the dark of the moon. You have to pay attention to the daily weather. With tomatoes it is essential to know the combination of temperature and humidity that fosters the tomato blight. This is the same blight that attacks the potato. It is the one that caused the Irish potato famine beginning in 1845, which decimated both the Irish potato harvest and the population. It helps explain why there are 35 million of us in the United States today who are of Irish descent—and why one-fourth of my DNA is Irish.

The attraction of systemic thinking influenced the academic path I chose to follow. The major in general agricultural science offered at Rutgers enabled me to take science courses in many fields. Taking a course, for example, in geology, meteorology, or genetics did not mean that I had much depth in these fields. But learning the basic concepts and vocabulary unique to each enabled me to look at issues from many different vantage points—something that would be invaluable in analyzing global environmental and food issues.

As a student, my record was well above average, but I was never interested in getting a PhD. For me, that was not the route to broadening my knowledge base. In the end, I settled for three degrees in three fields—agricultural science at Rutgers, agricultural economics at Maryland, and public administration at Harvard.

Free from the confines of a particular discipline, I am able to analyze the macro issues the world is facing in a systemic fashion, including such issues as climate change, population growth, food insecurity, the energy transition, and failing states. This approach has enabled me to sometimes see things others could not so easily see. In a world where specialization has become the norm, there is a hunger for a broader interdisciplinary understanding of the world's more pressing issues.

The positive feedback for taking this broader approach is itself rewarding. In April 2010 I was invited to participate in a panel discussion and screening on Capitol Hill of the popular movie *Avatar*, written and directed by James Cameron. Shortly after I arrived at the reception that preceded the panel, Cameron approached me and said, "I recognize you from your book jacket photo. I am reading *Plan B 4.0* for the fourth time." I was astounded.

During the panel discussion, which also included columnist Tom Friedman, actress Sigourney Weaver, and MSNBC's Joe Scarborough, Cameron—whose education was partly in the sciences—explained that he had only in recent years become interested in environmental issues. He found himself reading countless articles in scientific journals as well as news reports as he tried to piece together the big picture. He found it time-consuming and frustrating. And then a friend recommended that he read *Plan B 4.0*. It was just what Cameron needed. He could now see the big picture, the earth's ecosystem and its relationship with the global economic and political systems. He could understand, for example, how rising temperatures lower grain yields and how environmental degradation contributes to state failure.

Although many individuals have written books about the

environment, they tend to be one-time efforts, not an ongoing series. Against this backdrop, my books, roughly one per year, including the *State of the World* reports, represent the closest thing there is to a history of world environmental trends and developments for the last half of the twentieth century.

The lack of official tracking of environmental trends contrasts sharply with those of agriculture and health. The U.N. agencies that were formed during the early years of the United Nations were producing their own annual status reports. For example, the U.N. Food and Agriculture Organization published *The State of Food and Agriculture* each year. The World Health Organization produced *World Health Statistics*. Likewise, the International Labour Organization published an annual report on the status of the world's labor force.

The U.N. Environment Programme (UNEP) was not created until 1972. Headed initially by Maurice Strong, it was by U.N. standards a shoestring organization with a limited budget. It was not until 1997 that UNEP began publishing an occasional report entitled *Global Environment Outlook*. These are useful, information-rich reports, but only five of them have been published over the last fifteen years.

At the personal level, I take great pride in the achievements of my son and daughter. Shirley, who assumed much of the responsibility for raising Brian and Brenda, initially because of my demanding travel schedule during the USDA years, then later after we divorced, is an exceptional mother. She has also been wonderfully supportive of me, both when we were married and ever since.

During the summers when Brian was an environmental science major at the University of Colorado in Boulder, he worked as a river guide for rafting trips and developed a strong interest in kayaking. At age twenty-two, he entered a kayak slalom race on the Youghiogheny River in western Pennsylvania. Three years later he became a member of the U.S. Slalom Kayak Team. After retiring from international competition several years later, Brian sold canoes and kayaks in the Rocky Mountain states. A few years later, he parlayed his income from this into real estate in Durango, Colorado, where he now lives. Brian enjoys living close to the edge. He has ten "first runs" of rivers—eight in North America and two in Latin America, the latter two originating on the Bolivian Plateau and flowing northeast into the Amazon Basin. In descending one of these rivers through unbelievably rugged terrain, he said he felt like he was in a place where no human had been before.

Over the past five years, Brian has turned to nature photography. At his first public exhibition in a gallery in Durango, there was standing room only. Three of his sixteen photographs sold the day before the show opened. In his words, he tries to "capture the essence or emotional context of a subject." He writes, "Often to me the process is so engaging that I forget to breathe, and the world ceases to exist outside of my view finder." A stunning photo he took of Denali (Mt. McKinley) during a father-son trip to Alaska in July 2011 hangs in the conference room at the Earth Policy Institute.

One thing I could do with Brian and Brenda was to encourage participation in sports. In high school, Brenda was interested in track. However, her school, with perhaps a dozen students in her class, did not have a girl's track team. A math teacher took her under her wing, registering Brenda in regional and state track meets, even driving her to them. I coached long distance. One of the most exciting events came in a thirteen-school state championship track meet, where Brenda entered both the one- and two-mile races. She placed in both and as a result scored enough points to finish seventh out of the thirteen teams.

Although she did not win either event, she outscored six of the teams. I am a proud father!

Brenda earned a degree in microbiology from Colorado State University in Fort Collins, followed by a doctorate in veterinary science. As a vet she treats both small and large animals. The small animal practice is based in her clinic in Greeley, Colorado. The large animal practice covers the forty-mile stretch of ranch country that goes from Greeley north to the Wyoming border, an area where there are many cattle and few people.

Brenda is a pioneer in animal acupuncture and routinely uses it in her practice. She is also a certified human acupuncturist. She can treat a rancher and his horse during the same call.

She and her husband, Chris Haun, have three children: Bridget, now at the University of Wyoming, Lena in Pawnee High School, and Cash who is in kindergarten. She and Chris, who has a light construction business, also have a ranch. What I find so remarkable about Brenda is that she is simultaneously a vet, always on call, a mother, and a rancher.

With my son and daughter living in Colorado and my brother and sister in New Jersey, I usually divide the holidays between them. I typically spend a week in the summer with Brenda's family, Brian, and Shirley in Aspen, often when I am addressing a conference there, and enjoy the week over Christmas at Brenda's ranch.

Carl and his wife, Mary Lou, host a cookout on July 4 as well as Thanksgiving for the extended Brown family. My brother's home is on the edge of the farm where we grew up and that he and I own. Carl looks after our farm, where his daughter, Darlene, and her family now live. We rent the land to a nearby farmer to grow soybeans.

Marion and her husband, Bob, a former French teacher, live

along a pleasant wooded stream eleven miles east of the farm. Marion, like me, worked her way through college, graduating from the University of Maryland with a degree in art history, which she taught in high school. She and Bob started the Canvas Bag, an art supply and framing business in Bridgeton. They also have a small art gallery next door where they display the work of local artists. And since Bob is also a runner, we have run countless miles together over the rural roads where I grew up. We have also run several Cherry Blossom 10-Mile races.

Marion and Bob always host my visits to New Jersey. Marion deserves a gold medal for her daily oversight of our parents during their latter years. She is also the family event organizer and family genealogist, learning things about our roots that are of intense interest to me.

My companion, Maureen Kuwano Hinkle, was a widely respected environmental lobbyist from 1972 to 1999. Among other notable achievements, she is the godmother of the USDA Conservation Reserve Program, which led to the conversion of over 30 million acres of highly erodible cropland back to grass or trees. We share many interests. She has time to read books I would like to read, notably those dealing with history and biography. She enjoys going with me to conferences, particularly those held in places like Davos and Aspen. In addition to her intellect, she is also a great cook and goes out of her way to make life easy for me.

In my personal life, I have always sought simplicity and efficiency. This begins with not owning a car. I live in a one-bedroom condo on the top floor of an older apartment building that faces north, overlooking Rock Creek Park, with the National Cathedral in the distant background. During the summer solstice, I can watch the sun set on the spires of the cathedral. (My own Stonehenge.) With the zoo only a half mile up the creek, I can hear the lions roar early in the morning. The one-mile walk to work on a quiet residential street integrates some exercise into my day and affords me time for reflection and occasionally a fresh idea. There are scores of good restaurants, including almost every ethnic restaurant imaginable, within a twenty-minute walk of my apartment.

My time is devoted largely to reading and writing, with some for speaking and the associated travel. Anyone wanting to be a systemic global analyst has to read all the time. My reading day begins in the office at 7:30 a.m., just after I've started the coffee, by quickly scanning the *Washington Post, The New York Times, The Wall Street Journal*, and the *Financial Times*. Each day my colleagues gather a set of articles from newspapers, magazines, scientific journals, and the Internet for me to read. They occasionally pass on a book they think I need to see.

I devote my mornings to writing, seven days a week. Technically I rarely actually write anything, nor do I type. Instead I dictate. If I'm doing a book, I spend some time thinking about the table of contents and getting feedback from my colleagues, trying to get the structure clearly in mind. Then my colleagues collect information from a diverse array of sources for each of the chapters. I go through this material, making notes on an unlined letter-sized pad. Once that is complete, I dictate from the notes. In the next stage, I rework the dictated draft. When it is ready for review, my colleagues read and critique it, giving me excellent feedback.

My simple lifestyle is designed to provide as much room for research and writing as possible. As my colleagues know well, I wear the same style light-blue Oxford weave cotton shirts every day—short sleeves for summer, long sleeves for winter—with dark blue shorts in the summer, and navy blue corduroy trousers in the winter. No time wasted in selecting colors. And, when necessary, I clip on a bow tie that I carry in my suit pocket.

And I use energy frugally. Although air-conditioning units were installed when the 1929 vintage apartment building was renovated some thirty-five years ago, I prefer to open the windows and use the ceiling fans that I have in each room. Otherwise, I could not hear the birds sing in the park or the leaves rustle in the summer breeze.

In terms of health, I have been remarkably fortunate to date. I have not called in sick over the past half-century. Is this because of inherited DNA or because I so enjoy what I am doing? I don't know. Maybe both.

For exercise, in addition to walking to work, I also run. When I started running competitively sixty-five years ago as a fourteen-year-old sophomore, I was not the best distance runner in our high school. After fifty-six years of running, I finally achieved national ranking as a ten-miler, ranking fourth in the seventy to seventy-four age group. After entering the seventy-five to seventy-nine age group, I moved up to third place. Next is the eighty-and-up category. We will see. This is my "persistence pays" story.

My training regimen has typically involved running four miles two nights a week, sometimes ending with running up 800 stairs, two at a time, at the Woodley Park-Zoo Metro escalator. Back at the apartment after running, I do a quick round of push-ups, pull-ups, and sit-ups. On Saturdays I do a distance run in Rock Creek Park of nine to fifteen miles, the distance depending on where I am in my training cycle. Running provides a sense of well-being. Without running to maintain at least a minimum of physical conditioning, I could not maintain the schedule that I do.

For some twenty-five years, roughly 1965 to 1990, I also played touch football every Saturday from Labor Day to Memorial Day with an "over-the-hill" group. Setting aside the world's problems and concentrating only on winning a football game was enormously relaxing. If I had the time, I would still be playing football.

I have no desire to accumulate wealth beyond the savings needed to sustain me. Although I have received millions in speaking fees and prizes, I have always channeled this income into the organizations where I worked.

When I am asked by young people, often college students, for career advice, I usually suggest that they resist the trend in our educational system to become ever-more specialized as they progress up the educational ladder. Instead, I urge them to develop their own educational agenda, one that broadens their knowledge base. There are many specialists in the world, but what we desperately need now are people who can integrate across fields of knowledge and think broadly about the big issues.

Additional suggestions for students: Pursue your dream, set your standards high, and keep raising the bar. Don't fear failure. That is how we learn. And dream big. Goethe summed it up: "Dream no small dreams for they have no power to move the hearts of men."

What will my legacy be? Bryan Walker writing for Celsius. com in 2011 has described my role as follows: "Brown understands well the precariousness of human civilisation as the time of environmental reckoning draws ominously closer. He expresses it in patient and telling detail that addresses the intelligence and humanity of the reader. He equally buttresses his outline of the solutions with solid information as to how and why they can work. Whether sanity and clarity carry weight in the halls of power may be moot, but Brown well represents the thinking of the substantial body of people who see the perils ahead and want their governments to mobilise to avert them."

In my mind, helping to develop the concept of sustainable development is my principal legacy. Closely related to this is systemic thinking and analysis, a mode of research that became the foundations of both the Worldwatch and the Earth Policy institutes.

The concept of environmentally sustainable development began evolving in my mind during the early 1960s when I was writing *Man, Land and Food* and looking at the relationships between projected population growth and the earth's land and water resources. I began to see a troubling relationship emerging between growing human demands on the earth's natural systems—including forests, grasslands, fisheries, and croplands—and their carrying capacities. I was by no means the only one to work on this concept, but two of the books I wrote early on, *The Twenty-Ninth Day* in 1978 and *Building a Sustainable Society* in 1981, helped to further understanding of what sustainable development was and how to attain it.

As my thinking on sustainable development progressed, it evolved into Plan B, which not only describes a society that can endure but also how to create it. The development of Plan B with my colleagues at the Earth Policy Institute has been particularly rewarding as it allows me to draw on a lifetime of research. The good news is that more and more governments are recognizing that business as usual is no longer a viable option and that they need to adopt Plan B or something very similar to it.

The yardstick by which I judge myself is not in terms of how many books I've written, though that has been rewarding, or how many talks I've given, much as I've enjoyed them, but rather whether we are reversing the trends that are undermining our future. Are we making the transition from fossil fuels to wind, solar, and geothermal energy fast enough to prevent climate change from spiraling out of control? Are we reforesting the earth, reducing pollution, and stabilizing world population? If we cannot reverse the trends that have us on a decline-and-collapse scenario, I cannot claim success.

There are many developments that spawn hope. For example, in the United States, the world's largest economy, carbon emissions are falling fast as coal plants close and as cars become more fuel efficient. The Sierra Club's Beyond Coal campaign reports that more than one fourth of U.S. coal plants have closed or will soon do so. Their goal is to shutter every one.

The Obama administration has mandated a 50 percent reduction in fuel use of new cars between 2010 and 2025. Oil consumption in the United States, which is already falling, will continue to do so in the years ahead.

Following the crop-shrinking drought and heat in the United States during the summer of 2012 and Superstorm Sandy that ravaged New Jersey and New York in the fall of 2012, society is recognizing the need to take action on climate change. Once societies reach these tipping points, change can come very fast.

I am sometimes asked when I plan to retire. I have no plans to do so simply because I so enjoy what I am doing. There are still many trends to be reversed. My goal is to keep working as long as mind and body permit. If we can reverse these trends, we may be able to move civilzation onto a sustainable path. What could be more satisfying?

Acknowledgments

My personal indebtedness to others goes back to my early years. I thank Grandpop Smith who taught me to read at the age of four and Pop who took me to the gatherings around the cracker barrel at the general store where I learned to appreciate the art of telling stories.

I am indebted to my brother Carl who though three years younger always supported my teenage plans for ambitious farming projects. And my life would likely have followed a very different track had not Kathleen (Petri) Hoffmeyer nominated me for the International Farm Youth Exchange program that sent me to India.

At the U.S. Department of Agriculture I worked in an environment where the only constraints on what I could achieve were those imposed by my inherent personal limitations. For this I am indebted to my visionary branch chief Quentin West and to the entire chain of command—Wilhelm Anderson, Nate Koffsky, Joe Robertson, and John Schnittker—through to Secretary Orville Freeman.

Starting two environmental research institutes requires financial support. My thanks to William (Bill) Dietel of the Rockefeller Brothers Fund, who provided the half-million-dollar start-up grant for the Worldwatch Institute, and to Roger and Vicki Sant who did the same for the Earth Policy Institute (EPI).

I owe an unending debt of gratitude to Shirley Wiggin. Although our marriage lasted only fifteen years, she has been wonderfully supportive for half a century.

As ever, my thanks go to my sister Marion and her husband Bob who seemed to take delight in using their framing business and skills to frame my various awards and honorary degrees. They also provide strong personal support, including a place to stay whenever I go back home to Bridgeton. Bob is, in many ways, a brother.

In writing an autobiography, a genre quite out of my comfort zone, I relied on a number of people for reviewing various drafts. The hero awards for insightful feedback go to Maureen Kuwano Hinkle, Reah Janise Kauffman, and Janet Larsen. Thanks also to my EPI colleagues Matt Roney, Emily Adams, Hayley Moller, Sara Rasmussen, Julianne Simpson, Brigid Fitzgerald, and Millicent Johnson. Among my many friends whose suggestions have improved the manuscript are Miles Benson, Bill Dietel, Georgie Anne Geyer, Peter Goldmark, Judy Gradwohl, Linda Harrar, Scott McVay, Jim Risser, and Raisa Scriabine.

Over the last half-century, I have benefited enormously from remarkably able support people. Blondeen Gravely became my administrative assistant beginning in 1965. We worked together in one capacity or another for twenty-nine memorable years. My second anchor is Reah Janise Kauffman, who joined me in 1986 and now serves as both my right hand and as vice president of EPI, wearing more hats than I can count. She spent countless hours digging through dusty file boxes from the last half century in basement storage rooms to pull out material used in this book—and so often remembered what I could not. My heartfelt thanks.

I am indebted to our hardworking research team of Janet Larsen, Matt Roney, and Emily Adams who fact-checked my memory; Millicent Johnson who made PDFs of old board and grant reports, which made fact-checking easier; Kristina Taylor who compiled a translation matrix of my books in all languages; and Julianne Simpson who catalogued fifty-odd years of lectures.

Lasting thanks go to Linda Starke who edited the manuscript twice early in its evolution. Thanks also to Amy Cherry, vice president and senior editor at W. W. Norton & Company, one of the world's finest publishing houses. Her guidance was invaluable in shaping this book at every step along the way. And thanks to Anna Mageras who expertly shepherded the book through its various phases.

Illustrating a life with photographs is an onerous task. For maintaining a digital and hard copy record of much of my career, thanks to Reah Janise, whose foraging resulted in most of the photographs in this book. For family photographs, thanks go to my sister Marion.

I reserve a special thanks to Maureen Kuwano Hinkle, a friend for over fifty years, and my companion, for suggesting the title for this book and for so much more.

Raising global awareness of the challenges facing us has depended heavily on the publishers who have translated my books into over forty languages. Without you I could not reach a worldwide readership, motivating millions to work for a sustainable future. I am eternally grateful for your selfless dedication to our shared goals.

And finally, thanks to you who read my books. It would all have been in vain without you.

Index